Beethoven and the Lyric Impulse

Amanda Glauert revisits Beethoven's songs and studies his profound engagement with the aesthetics of the poets he was setting, particularly those of Herder and Goethe.

Beethoven and the Lyric Impulse offers readers a rich exploration of the poetical and philosophical context in which Beethoven found himself when composing songs. It also offers detailed commentaries on possible responses to specific songs, responses designed to open up new ways for performing, hearing and appreciating this provocative song repertoire.

This study will be of great interest to researchers of Beethoven, German song and the aesthetics of words and music.

Amanda Glauert was formerly Director of Programmes and Research at the Royal College of Music, UK.

Routledge Voice Studies

Series editors: Konstantinos Thomaidis and Ben MacPherson

The *Routledge Voice Studies* series offers a platform for rigorous discussion of voice across disciplines, practices and areas of interest. This series aims to facilitate the dissemination and cross-fertilisation of voice-related research to effectively generate new knowledge and fresh critical insights on voice, vocality, and voicing.

Composing for Voice
A Guide for Composers, Singers, and Teachers
Paul Barker

Voice Studies
Critical Approaches to Process, Performance and Experience
Konstantinos Thomaidis and Ben MacPherson

Training Actors' Voices
Towards an Intercultural/Interdisciplinary Approach
Tara McAllister-Viel

The Performative Power of Vocality
Virginie Magnat

Somatic Voices in Performance Research and Beyond
Christina Kapadocha

Beethoven and the Lyric Impulse
Essays on Beethoven Song
Amanda Glauert

www.routledge.com/Routledge-Voice-Studies/book-series/RVS

Beethoven and the Lyric Impulse

Essays on Beethoven Song

Amanda Glauert

Routledge
Taylor & Francis Group

LONDON AND NEW YORK

First published 2021
by Routledge
2 Park Square, Milton Park, Abingdon, Oxon OX14 4RN

and by Routledge
605 Third Avenue, New York, NY 10017

First issued in paperback 2022

Routledge is an imprint of the Taylor & Francis Group, an informa business

British Library Cataloguing-in-Publication Data
A catalogue record for this book is available from the British Library

Library of Congress Cataloging-in-Publication Data
A catalog record for this book has been requested

ISBN 13: 978–0–367–54472–0 (pbk)
ISBN 13: 978–0–367–46356–4 (hbk)
ISBN 13: 978–1–003–02842–0 (ebk)

DOI: 10.4324/9781003028420

Typeset in Bembo
by Apex CoVantage, LLC

Contents

Music examples

Series foreword

The claim that voice is everywhere might be a truism. Voice is predominant in interpersonal and technologically mediated communications and features prominently in discussions of identity, psychological development, and language acquisition. From theatrical performance to avant-garde or operatic singing, voice also offers aesthetic pleasure and, as is the case with rhetoric or journalism, it facilitates or imposes messages, arguments and beliefs. Voice is also a powerful metaphor. Feminist scholars have championed the female voice, cultural studies has lent an attentive ear to subaltern voices, and the voice of the people is central to debates around politics, media, activism, and religion. In the arts, voice is not merely an instrument to be perfected or enjoyed. Notions of the artist's voice or, occasionally, the author's voice permeate relevant discourses. Non-human or posthuman voices invite us to listen to animal voices, interactive voice recognition systems, and vocal synthesis effected in robotics labs.

But how does one account for such plurality and multiplicity? How is voice to be discussed from a scholarly perspective? How might we move beyond bifurcated concepts of the voice in performance studies, for example?

The first, but decisive, step would be to create platforms for rigorous discussion of voice across disciplines, practices, and areas of interest. The Routledge Voice Studies series offers precisely such a platform. In the last few years, attention given to voice has shifted from sporadic publications in disparate areas of enquiry to the epicentre of discourses in a variety of overlapping disciplines. This series aspires to facilitate the dissemination and cross-fertilisation of voice-related research and effectively generate new knowledge and fresh critical insights on voice, vocality, and voicing. To that end, we are delighted to include in the series of publications a variety of formats. We are equally interested in monographs, themed edited collections, student-focused anthologies and sourcebooks, revised and expanded editions of classic texts, and inter-medial and multimedial outputs. Our hope is that these varied structures will attract both practitioners and scholars as contributors, and find a readership among established and emergent researchers, students and artists.

We understand voice studies as a shifting landscape of questions and concerns, as a proliferative inter-discipline. Building on current initiatives, we wish to expand and capitalise on the productive debates taking place in the areas of music, theatre, and performance studies, as well as cultural studies, ethnomusicology, sound studies, acoustics and acoustemology. Yet we are equally as keen on extending an invitation to inputs from psychology, fine art, poetics and orality studies, linguistics, media and film studies, robotics and artificial intelligence, history and philosophy, translation and adaptation studies, among others. Spearheaded by the discussions across disciplines and cultures hosted in its inaugural publication, the edited collection *Voice Studies: Critical Approaches to Process, Performance and Experience*, this book series listens out for new spaces in which voice can reverberate with revitalised vigour. We hope you enjoy this fascinating journey with us.

Series editors: Dr Konstantinos Thomaidis
and Dr Ben Macpherson

Introduction

It might seem provocative to include a study of Beethoven's songs in a series exploring voice and vocality. The genre of lyric song is defined first and foremost as an invitation to the listener to join in with the physical immediacy of singing, yet Beethoven often seems ill at ease with the limitations that come with writing for the human voice. Even as a rising artist in Vienna, the composer was visiting the Italian operatic composer Salieri for lessons in how to set words to music. His technical problems with the nooks and crannies of how the voice works seem to have been accompanied by aesthetic inhibitions. E. T. A. Hoffmann characterises Beethoven in his famous review of the Fifth Symphony as a composer for whom the finite 'external sensual world' is overtaken by the infinite (Strunk, 1981, 35). According to Hoffmann it is thus inevitable that he 'has less success with vocal music, which excludes the character of indefinite yearning' (Strunk, 1981, 37). Wagner would agree. In his essay 'Music of the Future' he heralds Beethoven as the composer who replaces melody with 'melos'. Melody often follows the shapes and rhythms of human breath and the exertions of enunciating syllables and phrases. 'Melos' allows another kind of utterance to emerge: rhythms of the forest – as Wagner terms them. Such an utterance 'will be forever resounding in [the listener's] mind, though he will never be able to hum it' (Jacobs, 1979, 41). For Schopenhauer too, Beethoven gives voice to emotions that transcend the particularity of 'flesh and bone'. Instead he offers a 'true and complete picture of the nature of the world', form without material, spirit without matter (Schopenhauer, 1958, 450).

In Schopenhauer's view, such a cosmic imagination belongs with the symphonic power of instruments; he clearly no longer takes the actual or implied presence of a human voice as the locus for the composer's appeal to listeners. To do so might compromise Schopenhauer's claims for Beethoven's genius and even competence as a composer. The poet Ludwig Tieck, in his short story 'Musical Sorrows and Joys' of 1822, is merciless in his characterisation of the mess Beethoven makes of song-writing, particularly in setting Goethe's lyrics: 'what restlessness, what sharp declamation, what darting from one idea to the next is evident in these works' (Siegel, 1983, 113). Such developmental instincts place the singing performer at a disadvantage, but so too the listener who is not allowed to 'enjoy one musical idea for any length of time'. Tieck implies that Beethoven disrupts the link between listeners' imaginative holding of breath as they contemplate a lyric idea – an idea caught in words and music – and the singer's physical spinning of breath.

Goethe celebrates the importance of this intimate sharing of breath between performer and listener in his poem *An Lina* (Goethe, 1800):

> Liebchen, kommen diese Lieder
> Jemals wieder dir zu Hand,
> Sitze beim Klaviere nieder,
> Wo der Freund sonst bei dir stand.

> Lass die Saiten rasch erklingen,
> Und dann sieh ins Buch hinein;
> Nur nicht lesen! immer singen!
> Und ein jedes Blatt ist dein.

> Ach, wie traurig sieht in Lettern,
> Schwarz auf weiss, das Lied mich an,
> Das aus deinem Mund vergöttern,
> Das ein Herz zerreissen kann!

> [Beloved, should these songs
> Ever return to your hand,
> Sit down at the keyboard,
> Where your friend used to stand beside you.

> Let the strings quickly sound,
> And then look into the book;
> Only don't read! Always sing!
> And every sheet will be yours.

> Oh, how sadly the letters,
> Black on white, look at me,
> That your mouth can deify,
> And break open the heart!]

(Author's translation)

An Lina has been called a manifesto for lyric song because of the power that is given to the singer's 'mouth' to break open the listener's heart (Wellbery, 1996, 211). The music on the stand, the seat at the keyboard, set the stage for the enlivening breath of the singer. The poet empties himself of voice – his poem is just the sad letters on the page – so that other, more immediate voices can be released. His role is to invoke the memory of a previous performance when poet and singer were together. Once the singer has brought the past into the present by 'breaking open the heart', the listener is primed to create a new memory ready for a further song reincarnation. The poet is just one among a community of lyricists, each moving between giving voice and eliciting voice. The lyric is inhabited by 'potentially multiple musical voices' – to use the terms of Carolyn Abbate (1991, x) – some heard and some imagined. The physicality of the singer's breakthrough moment, the 'I sing' which Herder saw as defining the lyric (Chamberlain, 1992, 127), is celebrated by the listener's response as well as by the singer's power. The silence of listening back to the singer's voice, or sounding the keyboard's strings in expectation as referred to in *An Lina*, might create as much sympathetic resonance as the impact of the human voice itself.

From such a point of view Beethoven's ease with an instrument, with a piano rather than the human voice, should not of itself disqualify him as a song-maker. Treating the voice and sung words merely as a filler for symphonic development might do so, but using the instrument to invoke echoes of song and singing would not. Much of the distinction lies with listener-performers, with whether they are willing to listen out for empathetic resonances of songs and singing in Beethoven's music. It might be hard to reposition Beethoven from the lone symphonist to a vocally inspired collaborator, but even the existence of his large body of songs should make one pause. Many of the songs offer evidence of Beethoven's deep engagement with sung words, not just with the physical realities of working with the rhythms of vocal production, but also with what those rhythms represent – the possibility of the listener joining in and making a community of responses. In his songs one can see and hear evidence of the lyric impulse, where the roles of words and music, production and reception, become inextricably linked, even to the point of becoming interchangeable. Thus calling Beethoven a vocalist or a voice-inspired composer should not necessarily be a contradiction in terms, provided one is open to the redefinitions of voice and vocality that come from delving into the songs themselves.

Those immediately responsible for summing up Beethoven's legacy were not always as definite as E. T. A. Hoffmann or Tieck in separating out his achievements as instrumental rather than vocal. When the poet Franz Grillparzer sought to sum up Beethoven's achievements, in an oration at the composer's graveside, he called him 'the last master of resounding song'. According to Grillparzer, Beethoven is a Behemoth who exhausts everything music might be said to express, from 'the cooing of doves' to 'the lawless violence of the striving forces of Nature'. No one will be able to follow such eloquence; music will have to start again. And yet Grillparzer identifies one artist who not only outlives Beethoven, but also in some sense matches and even contains him: Goethe. If he sees Beethoven as one half of the 'flower of the country's spirit', the other half is Goethe, the 'hero of poetry in the German language' (Grillparzer, 1964, 881–883; Hamburger, 1951, 269–270). Grillparzer compliments the composer by comparing him to a poet, but with this he also qualifies notions of his limitless power. With the phrase 'resounding song' he evokes specific ideals of the lyric impulse, where poetry and music are bound together as night follows day. If Beethoven's music as a whole is to be dubbed 'song' it should not just be celebrated for itself, it should also be valued as the resonance or outworking of poetry.

There are many reasons for seeing Grillparzer's way of celebrating Beethoven as provocative. Beethoven and Goethe were hardly congenial partners in their immediate dealings with each other. Whilst Beethoven was annoyed with Goethe for his lack of freedom in dealing with the aristocracy (Brandenburg, 1996, 287), Goethe criticised Beethoven for being an untamed force (Hecker, 1913, 328; Byrne Bodley, 2009, 156). As will be discussed in Chapter 1, Goethe's rejection of Beethoven's way of setting his poem 'Kennst du das Land' shows their personality differences extending into aesthetic matters. Goethe believed a musical setting should lift a poem like hot air within a balloon (Hecker, 1913, 59; Byrne Bodley, 2009, 266); Beethoven said he wanted his music to rise above the poem (Hamburger, 1951, 223). Both artists use the metaphor of music rising up, but one sees the ascent as taking the poem with it and the other as leaving it behind. According to Grillparzer, Beethoven also talked about envying poets' wider sphere of activity (Hamburger, 1951, 268). This suggests his respect for poetry, but if the endpoint was to replace the poet, then he might have been wishing to free himself from the need to rely on others' words once and for all. The words of the baritone soloist that announce the entry of Schiller's poetry in the finale of Beethoven's Ninth Symphony are, after all, the composer's own.

Beethoven is even reported by Friedrich Rochlitz as saying, 'I am not keen on writing songs' (Hamburger, 1951, 186). It is difficult to know what to make of this statement. Why, then, did he write so many? Paul Reid includes some 140 items in his *Beethoven Song Companion*. The arguments that he needed to show his proficiency in all musical genres or that he was fulfilling occasional functions hardly explain the depth and breadth of this body of music. Bettina von Arnim provides a fanciful answer with the words she imagines coming from Beethoven's mouth:

> Goethe's poems exercise great power over me, not only by their content, but by their rhythm. His language is such that it stimulates me and puts me in a mood to compose, for, as if with the aid of spirits, it attains a higher order and contains the secret of harmony within it. So, from the focal point of enthusiasm, I must discharge melody in all directions. I pursue it, passionately catch up with it again, see it flee from me and vanish in a crowd of excitements; now I seize it with renewed passion, cannot bear to part with it, must multiply it in all its modulations in a quick ecstasy, and at the last moment I triumph over the first musical idea. You see, that's a symphony.
>
> (Hamburger, 1951, 88)

From Bettina's standpoint, Beethoven's songs can be seen as experiments in melodic generation, as part of the composer's sketching processes. She suggests that the prop of working with a poet's rhythms and images becomes thrown away as the composer discovers his own way of bringing together time and space, detail and whole. Joseph Kerman implies such a notion when he calls Beethoven's song-cycle *An die ferne Geliebte* 'a quiet herald of the late style' (Tyson, 1973, 154). A herald announces the glories to come, and a 'quiet' herald is certainly not meant to draw attention to itself.

Song-writing is not usually seen as an important part of Beethoven's late style, even though many interesting songs come from that period, as discussed in Chapter 4. This may be because songs, even songs extended into a song-cycle, are seen as too slight to carry the discursive philosophical weight associated with the composer's late period. In their discussion of Beethoven's late style, Joseph Kerman and Michael Spitzer speak of the influence of 'lyricism' but not of the 'lyric' or 'lyric song' as such (Kerman, 1966, 195–196; Spitzer, 2006, 117, 119, 125). Lyric song is often associated with an adherence to particular dimensions of scale, with detailed attention to metre and word-setting and to precise patterns of repetition at the level of line or stanza. Yet, according to Goethe's teacher Johann Gottfried Herder, poetry should not be treated as a matter of genre but as 'effect on our soul, energy' (Chamberlain, 1992, 131). Herder defines the lyric as the point where one can sense the artist stepping towards the listener with the appeal, 'I sing!' (127). Homer and Shakespeare are two of Herder's foremost singing lyricists, though one works with the epic and the other with drama. Aristotle associates the

terms epic and drama with definite external characteristics; he believes
the drama implies singleness of action and precision of denouement (Halliwell, 1987, 40), whilst the epic allows 'scope for considerable extension
of length and multiple plot-structures' (Halliwell, 1987, 59). The lyric is
not included as a third type of structuring, only as a form of 'garnishing'
(Halliwell, 1987, 38). As Emil Staiger notes, Goethe and Schiller also
draw back from adding the lyric to their discussion of generic principles
(1991, 72). Its omission from Aristotle's *Poetics* might have been incidental, but it also seems appropriate if one agrees with Herder that the lyric
has to be defined internally. For him, lyric is in essence a performance or
listening term, implying the different kind of attention to time and space
that occurs as one invokes the action of picking up the lyre.

If Herder hears the lyric impulse, the 'I sing!', as governing both
Homer and Shakespeare's epic and dramatic creations, then one might
claim the same for listening to Beethoven's symphonic music. Indeed, his
very struggle with writing songs could be taken as a sign of the strength
of his lyric impulses, ones that refuse to be generically bound but seek to
resonate as widely as possible. Resonance was a key concept in Herder's
description of what singing to the lyre entails:

> The plucked chord performs its natural duty – it sounds! It calls
> for an echo from one that feels alike, even if there is no one there.
> Nature hides sounds in these chords which, when called forth and
> encouraged, can communicate, as though along an invisible chain.
>
> (Herder, 1986, 87)

One can sense immediate points of sympathy here with Beethoven's
abiding concern to reach a 'distant beloved'; 'from the heart may it go
the heart' he writes over the score of *Missa Solemnis* (Cooper, 1996, 256).
The question is, perhaps, how this calling forth of response best happens.
Herder often associates the appeal of the lyric impulse with unexpected
effort or even violence. In contrast to soothing images of Orpheus and
his lute, attracting flowers and animals in his wake, Herder summons up
the image of Ossian, whose songs command attention through a kind of
rough force:

> The purpose, the nature, the miraculous power of these songs as
> the delight, the driving force, the traditional chant, and everlasting
> joy of the people – all this depends on the lyrical, living dance-like
> quality of the song, on the living presence of the images, and the
> coherence and, as it were, compulsion of the content, the feelings;
> on the symmetry of the words and syllables, and sometimes even of

the letters, on the flow of the melody, and on a hundred other things that belong to the living world, to the gnomic song of the nation, and vanish with it. These are the arrows of the barbarous Apollo with which he pierces our heart and transfixes soul and memory.

(Chamberlain, 1992, 134–135)

According to Herder, this 'barbarous Apollo' sends out sounds like arrows. Later in this essay on the songs of ancient people, he praises Ossian for harnessing the energy of 'alliterative syllables', which are offered as 'signals for the metrical beat, marching orders to the warrior band' (Chamberlain, 1992, 135). This energy comes from a compression of sound, not expansion, as the ear is drawn to the 'symmetry of the words and syllables, and sometimes even of the letters'. The sound is collected and imprinted on the senses at the point of vanishing, of contracting into the merest breath. For, according to *Chambers English Dictionary* (1988), with the notion of 'syllables' comes the notion of what can be 'uttered by a single effort of the voice'. Here the lyric impulse finds its most literal expression, as an effortful expulsion of air that corresponds to the physicality of plucking the lyre, a single action which prompts repetition. The Ossianic singer starts the process – with the 'signal' of rhyming alliteration – but the full resonance of the action comes from others joining in. Herder often speaks of Ossianic song being characterised by 'Sprünge und Würfe' (leaps and throws), by an energy that not only moves in spurts but leaves gaps which the listener has to fill in, as it were (Chamberlain, 1992, 140). Ossian never existed in the literal sense, but Herder refuses to give up on the possibility of the continuing power of Ossianic-style song since it draws on immediate responses to physical acts of singing:

> The longer the song is to last, the stronger and the more attached to the senses these arousers of the soul must be to defy the power of time and the changes of the centuries.
>
> (Chamberlain, 1992, 135)

If one looks at the two settings of Herder's poems that Beethoven made in his later period, the Ossianic tribute leaps off the page though in such miniature guise that little attention has been paid to them. No one tends to sing these songs, with the exception of those who are committed to exploring the whole of Beethoven's song repertoire. The question of context is indeed puzzling. It is possible that such songs belong more in a communal sing-song session, as in a club or a salon, than in a solo Lieder recital. But most inhibiting for singers is perhaps the question of whether Beethoven really valued these songs and 'meant' them, in the way he clearly 'meant' his late piano bagatelles, for example. As will be discussed in Chapter 4, one can approach these songs as a serious tribute to Herder and to his belief that a composer should restrict himself to the power of simple folk-like song. But such an exercise in musical kenosis can sit strangely with what else one knows about Beethoven and his music.

In the year of making the first of his two Herder settings, 1813, Beethoven quoted these words from the poet in his *Tagebuch*: 'Speech is like silver, but to be silent at the right moment is pure gold' (Solomon, 1988, 247). For Herder, silence is integral to the release of the lyric impulse. As he noted in his essay *On the Origin of Language*, man is foremost 'a listening and noting creature' (Herder, 1986, 129). Herder imagines Adam having the shock of first hearing a sheep 'baa' in the Garden of Eden and being reduced to an uncomfortable silence, but then listening and gathering the 'ringing sound' into a 'distinguishing mark' so that he can bleat back: 'You are that which goes baa' (Herder, 1986, 117).

> Even if the occasion were never to arise for him that he should want or be able to transmit this idea to another human being . . . his soul – as it were – bleated within when it selected this sound as a sign of recollection, and it bleated again as it recognised the sound by its sign. . . .
>
> (Herder, 1986, 118)

Through giving the role of sound-creator to a sheep, Herder indicates that the weight of any utterance comes from the response of others. The sheep is hardly able to proclaim the 'I sing', but in the process of others 'baa-ing' back, a moment of utterance becomes celebrated and prolonged through an 'invisible chain' of responses (Herder, 1986, 87).

When Goethe sets up Mignon, the child-like figure of his novel *Wilhelm Meisters Lehrjahre*, as a perfect lyricist, it is precisely for her uncanny ability to work on the hearts of others. Her appeal to silence and her extreme reticence link her to Herder's essential view of man as a 'listening and noting creature'. Her lyrics speak of what cannot be expressed except through an appeal to another's sympathetic response. The question of how much Beethoven was able to respond in kind to the challenge of Mignon's mode of singing might be taken as a test of the nature of his own lyric impulse. For this reason Chapter 1 will discuss in detail the evidence for and against including Beethoven in the chain of sympathetic respondents to Mignon. It might be foolhardy to claim that Beethoven understood Mignon better than Goethe himself. But in exploring the many layers that surround the figure and her mode of lyric expression, the chapter seeks to create a sense of context for Beethoven's provocative interpretation. Chapter 2 adds further perspective to Beethoven's Mignon settings by relating them to the sequence of 'distant beloved' songs that spreads over a significant part of the composer's song output. The climax and summary of such poetic material in Beethoven's song-cycle *An die ferne Geliebte* offers an opportunity for enquiring where Beethoven arrived in song. The sequence bears the distinctive hallmarks of a concern for lyric song such as can be applied to an understanding of other songs, both those by Beethoven and those by other composers. These models can also be applied to some of the instrumental music of the late period, as discussed in Chapter 3. In works such as the Ninth Symphony and the Op. 130 String Quartet, Beethoven comes close to defining a lyric as against a dramatic or epic impulse. The usual progression of seeing Beethoven's lyric impulse as a stepping-stone to the drama of his instrumental music is here reversed, with lyric song being approached as an arrival-point in the composer's compositional journey. Chapter 4 approaches the question of the status of Beethoven song, from the point of view of individual late songs where the question of miniaturism comes to the fore. Here the issue is whether a song can be approached as an endpoint even when the slightness of the material might seem to discourage such an evaluation. From comparisons with Mahler and Wolf, the chapter seeks to show how Beethoven's song distillations can offer far-reaching insights into how the lyric is understood – across the corpus of the German Lied and beyond.

Exploration of song is always a collaborative enterprise. I would never have come to write this book without the inspiration of all the performers I have had the joy of working with, both in connection with the Lyric Song Salon which I ran with colleagues at the Royal Academy of Music for many years, and with SONGART, the research group convened by myself, Kathryn Whitney and Paul Barker, and hosted by the Institute of Musical Research at the University of London. I am particularly grateful to singers April Fredrick, Alison Pearce, Cerys Jones, Norbert Meyn, Kathryn Whitney and Nicholas Clapton for helping find new voices in Beethoven. Yet I hope they will forgive me for saying that some of the best 'singing' I ever heard came from pianist colleagues, Aaron Shorr, Alban Coombs, Paul Barker, Natasha Loges, Briony Williams Cox, Imma Setiadi and Andrew West, in a contradiction that tells a great deal about the challenge of performing Beethoven song.

References

Abbate, Carolyn. *Unsung Voices*. Princeton, NJ: Princeton University Press, 1991.

Brandenburg, Sieghard (ed.). *Beethoven-Briefwechsel*. Volume 2. Munich, Germany: Henle, 1996.

Byrne Bodley, Lorraine (ed.). *Goethe and Zelter: Musical Dialogues*. London: Ashgate, 2009.

Chamberlain, Timothy J. (ed.). *Eighteenth Century German Criticism*. New York: Continuum, 1992.

Chambers English Dictionary. Cambridge: Cambridge University Press, 1988.

Cooper, Barry (ed.). *The Beethoven Compendium*. London: Thames and Hudson, 1996.

Goethe, Johann Wolfgang von. *Neue Schriften*. Volume 7. Berlin: Johann Friedrich Unger, 1800.

Grillparzer, Franz. *Sämtliche Werke*. Volume 2, ed. Peter Frank and Karl Pörnbacher. Munich, Germany: Carl Hanser, 1964.

Halliwell, Stephen. *The Poetics of Aristotle*. London: Duckworth, 1987.

Hamburger, Michael (ed.). *Beethoven: Letters, Journals and Conversations*. London: Thames and Hudson, 1951.

Hecker, Max (ed.). *Der Briefwechsel zwischen Goethe and Zelter*. Volume 1. Leipzig, Germany: Insel Verlag, 1913.

Herder, Johann Gottfried. *On the Origin of Language*, tr. John H. Moran and Alexander Gode. Chicago: Chicago University Press, 1986.

Jacobs, Robert L. (tr.). *Three Wagner Essays*. London: Ernst Eulenberg, 1979.

Kerman, Joseph. *The Beethoven Quartets*. New York: W.W. Norton, 1966.

Reid, Paul. *The Beethoven Song Companion*. Manchester: Manchester University Press, 2007.

Schopenhauer, Arthur. *The World as Will and Representation*. Volume 2, tr. E.F.J. Payne. New York: Dover Publications, 1958.

Siegel, Linda (ed. and tr.). *Music in German Romantic Literature*. Novato, CA: Elra Publications, 1983.

Solomon, Maynard. *Beethoven Essays*. Cambridge, MA: Harvard University Press, 1988.

Spitzer, Michael. *Music as Philosophy: Adorno and Beethoven's Late Style*. Bloomington and Indianapolis: Indiana University Press, 2006.

Staiger, Emil. *Basic Concepts of Poetics*, ed. Marianne Burkhard and Luanne T. Frank, tr. Janette C. Hudson and Luanne T. Frank. University Park, PA: Pennsylvania State University Press, 1991.

Strunk, Oliver (ed.). *Source Readings in Music History: The Romantic Era*. London: Faber and Faber, 1981.

Tyson, Alan (ed.). *Beethoven Studies*. New York: W.W. Norton, 1973.

Wellbery, David, E. *The Specular Moment: Goethe's Early Lyric and the Beginnings of Romanticism*. Stanford: Stanford University Press, 1996.

1 Do you know the land

The challenge of singing Mignon

In the Pasqualati House of the Vienna Museum hangs a portrait by Joseph Mähler of Beethoven from the period 1804–1805; it shows the composer supposedly confronting his deafness by holding a lyre-guitar in one hand whilst the other reaches out to his imaginary audience. Storm clouds gather in the background to threaten the pastoral scene, which the outlines of cypresses and a temple suggest should be Arcadia. Beethoven is portrayed as a slightly forbidding Orpheus, both attracting and repelling his listeners with his music. Owen Jander has indeed linked this portrait to the defiant character of Beethoven's Fifth Symphony, where the restless energy of instrumental rhythms overshadows vocally derived melody. This Orpheus, with the raised right hand, promises to declaim rather than sing perhaps; the lyre is present only as a prop, and possibly a quite incongruous one. Jander points out that one string from the lyre-guitar is missing, the highest one, as though to symbolise what Beethoven can no longer hear (Jander, 2008, 25–70). Yet the composer is portrayed as defying any limitation; he desires to push on from Arcadia without a backwards glance it seems.

Goethe's response on hearing Mendelssohn perform Beethoven's Fifth Symphony for him at the piano was that a destructive force had indeed been unleashed, one that he feared would bring the house down around his ears (Goethe, 1966, 221). It is difficult to know whether Goethe's comment suggests admiration or criticism. Grillparzer's description of Beethoven as a sea monster, in his oration at the composer's grave, certainly implies appreciation: 'As Behemoth rushes, tempestuous over the oceans, so he flew over the frontiers of his art' (Grillparzer, 1964, 882; Hamburger, 1951, 269–270). Schopenhauer too praises Beethoven for creating a 'true and complete picture of the nature of the world, which rolls on in the boundless confusion of innumerable forms, and maintains itself by constant destruction' (Schopenhauer, 1958, 450). Such a notion of rushing forwards accords well with the aesthetics of symphonic composition but not so well with song. When associated with Arcadia, song implies tuning in to what has already been sung. Goethe disliked the notion of 'composed', preferring that of 'sounded' (Eckermann, 1970, 415; Schwab, 1965, 44; Moser, 1949, 92); songs should thus give the impression of having always existed and of just needing fresh details of connection. In his novel *Wilhelm Meisters Lehrjahre*, Goethe shows his eponymous hero being wooed by different types of singer, from the artless and superficial Philine to the burdened Harper. Though the Harper's singing moves Wilhelm immensely, he is presented as sometimes lapsing into incoherence under the effort to sing what has never been sung before. He might be taken as a warning of the dangers of trusting to music alone, or specifically to the powers of composing rather than those of listening and performing.

The Harper is one of the supreme figures of musical Romanticism. From his first private scene with Wilhelm, Goethe creates a deeply sympathetic picture of an artist struggling to weave together 'well known and unknown songs and snatches, and thereby set moving a complex of recent and more remote feelings, waking and slumbering, pleasant and painful emotions' (Goethe, 1995, 79). The Harper's poems are introduced as the product of his 'rhapsodizing, repeating stanzas, half singing, half reciting' (Goethe, 1995, 77). They are not presented as songs that can be sung back by others; it is made clear that all is newly composed in the moment, and also disappears with the moment so that the Harper remains a 'stranger everywhere' (Goethe, 1995, 78). Whilst the Harper is a powerful symbol of the artist as restless wanderer, Goethe creates an alternative picture of song through the figure of Mignon. In her most famous lyric 'Kennst du das Land', she uses her refrain – 'You know it, yes?' – to suggest that Arcadia should be a present as well as a past reality. The land she refers to may be identified with specific features of Italy and with aspects of her personal history – her history of exile and abduction as revealed later in the novel (Goethe, 1995, 320). But with her urgent refrain Mignon appeals to her listener to find the archetypes that underlie the poem's three stanzas, the three scenes which unfold like images of before and after the Fall:

Kennst du das Land, wo die Zitronen blühn,
Im dunkleln Laub die Gold-Orangen glühn,
Ein sanfter Wind vom blauen Himmel weht,
Die Myrte still und hoch der Lorbeer steht,
Kennst du es wohl?

Dahin! Dahin
Möcht ich mit dir, o mein Geliebter, ziehn.

Kennst du das Haus? Auf Säulen ruht sein Dach,
Es glänzt der Saal, es schimmert das Gemach,
Und Marmorbilder stehn und sehn mich an:
Was hat man dir, du armes Kind, getan?
Kennst du es wohl?
Dahin! Dahin
Möcht ich mit dir, o mein Beschützer, ziehn.

Kennst du den Berg und seinen Wolkensteg?
Das Maultier sucht im Nebel seinen Weg,
In Höhlen wohnt der Drachen alte Brut,
Es stürzt der Fels und über ihn die Flut;
Kennst du es wohl?
Dahin! Dahin
Geht unser Weg! o Vater, laß uns ziehn!

(Goethe, 1994, 132)

[Know you the land where lemon blossoms blow,
And through dark leaves the golden oranges glow,
A gentle breeze wafts from an azure sky,
The myrtle's still, the laurel tree grows high –
You know it, yes? Oh there, oh there
With you, O my beloved, would I fare.

Know you the house? Roof pillars over it,
The chambers shining and the hall bright-lit,
The marble figures gaze at me in rue:
"You poor poor child, what have they done to you?"
You know it, yes? Oh there, oh there
With you, O my protector, would I fare.

Know you the mountain and its cloudy trails?
The mule picks out its path through misty veils,
The dragon's ancient brood haunts caverns here,
The cliff drops straight, the stream above falls sheer.
You know it, yes? Oh there, oh there
Our path goes on! There, Father, let us fare!]

(Goethe, 1995, 83)

The first stanza of Mignon's lyric is closely modelled on lines from James Thomson's 'Summer':

> Bear me, Pomona! to thy citron groves;
> To where the lemon and the piercing lime,
> With the deep orange, glowing through the green,
> Their lighter glories blend. Lay me, reclin'd,
> Beneath the spreading tamarind, that shakes,
> Fann'd by the breeze, its fever-cooling fruit.
>
> (Sternfeld, 1954, 34)

Goethe echoes Thomson's lilting iambic pentameter rhythms and the images of citron groves, but underlying both poetic scenes is the promise of a garden that brings communion with the beloved, as set out in Chapter 4 of the Bible's Song of Songs. The list of heady scents and colours is reminiscent of the description of delights that Solomon's bride offers to her bridegroom:

> You are a garden locked up, my sister, my bride;
> You are a spring enclosed, a sealed fountain.
> Your plants are an orchard of pomegranates
> With choice fruits, with henna and nard,
> Nard and saffron, calamus and cinnamon,
> With every kind of incense tree,
> With myrrh and aloes and all the finest spices.
>
> (*New International Version*, 2011, 682)

As in Song of Songs, Goethe and Thomson's poems call on the effect of the breeze to release the smells to the senses:

> Awake, north wind, and come south wind!
> Blow on my garden, that its fragrance may spread everywhere spices.
>
> (*New International Version*, 2011, 683)

Such an evocation is designed to transcend personal memories. The reference to the beloved – 'mein Geliebter' – at the close of Mignon's first stanza suggests a generic name for a responsive listener, rather than simply Wilhelm, just as the title 'Mignon' suggests 'darling' rather than a specific name. With her first verse, in particular, Mignon could be quoting any song from a darling to a beloved. Goethe's reference to Mignon's accompanying herself with a zither suggests a popular version of the lyre, the zither being an instrument for people to dance to. In the scene where

Mignon sings 'Kennst du das Land', in Chapter 1 of Book 3 of his novel, Goethe emphasises the performance qualities of her rendering, as she encourages an immediate response from her listener:

> She intoned each verse with a certain solemn grandeur, as if she were drawing attention to something unusual and imparting something of importance. When she reached the third line, the melody became more somber; the words 'You know it, yes?' were given weightiness and mystery, the 'Oh there, oh there!' were suffused with longing, and she modified the phrase 'Let us fare!' each time it was repeated, so that one time it was entreating and urging, the next time pressing and full of promise.
>
> (Goethe, 1995, 84)

The differences in performance between being 'entreating and urging' and 'pressing and full of promise' are not immediately apparent. It is also not clear which style would be most suitable for each of the three verses of the poem. The readers have to try out possibilities in their heads. Thus Goethe offers a scene that is not just *about* performance, but *for* performance. The poem is put at the head of the chapter, so that after reading the performance description below, the reader is encouraged to turn back and reread the poetic text bearing in mind what Mignon is said to have done. In fact, Goethe suggests Mignon performs the song three times in the course of the scene, once outside the door of Wilhelm's room, once inside the door, and once so that Wilhelm can try to capture it and write it down:

> Some hours later [Wilhelm] recognized music outside his door, and assumed at first that this was the Harper; but he heard the sound of a zither and the voice that began to sing was Mignon's. He opened the door for Mignon who came in and sang the song we have just communicated. The melody and the expression pleased Wilhelm greatly, though he could not make out all the words. So he asked her to repeat it, and explain it; then he wrote it down and translated it into German. He found, however, that he could not even approximate the originality of the phrases, and the childlike innocence of the style was lost when the broken language was smoothed over and the disconnectedness removed. The charm of the melody was also quite unique.
>
> (Goethe, 1995, 83)

Wilhelm clearly fails to capture the charm of Mignon's song. The words on the page do not do justice to her. It is doubtful whether the musical insert in the original edition, of a setting by Reichardt, is able to do justice to her either. It clearly did not offend Goethe, unlike the efforts of Beethoven and Spohr. But, as his words on Beethoven's and Spohr's settings make clear, the most crucial issue for Goethe seems to be not what composers do when singing Mignon but what they should avoid:

> It seems strange to me that both Beethoven and Spohr so completely misunderstood the song when they composed it. The distinctive mark in the same place in each verse, I would think, was enough to tell composers that what I expect from them is simply a song. Evidently, Mignon by her very nature could not sing an aria, but only a song.
>
> (Němec, 1941, 239; Byrne, 2004, 170)

The appeal to the diegesis of what Mignon might be able to sing seems strange in the context of a novel rather than a play. The Mignon of *Wilhelm Meister* is so clearly a figure of fantasy, shifting in appearance between boy and girl, girl and woman, that the reference to 'her nature' is highly provocative. Goethe himself continues to play games with the question of her identity when he suggests meeting a Mignon-like figure in the 11-year-old daughter of a harper on his travels to Italy in 1786 (Goethe, 1982, 28). Thinking of what an 11-year-old would be capable of singing certainly underlines the notion of 'childlike innocence' in Mignon's performance. But the point is surely that readers must be given space to seek out an aural persona for Mignon for themselves from the various ingredients that are presented to them. With each ingredient the mystery of how Mignon sounds becomes more acute. Even the insertion of the Reichardt setting in the first edition of the novel does little to end speculation. Reichardt resists giving a memorable musical version of the poem's 'distinctive mark', the refrain; indeed, overall, the song conveys little sense of a catchy tune. Instead the setting comes across as a written out improvisation, fluid and even declamatory in style, as emphasised by the performance instruction 'mit Affekt' (Reichardt, n.d.)(see Example 1.1).

Within the setting Reichardt creates a series of musical gestures that can map quite precisely onto the five stages indicated in Mignon's performance:

Stage (1) 'Solemn grandeur': bars 1 to 8 (spacious rise and fall of matching two and   four-bar phrases within a broad eight-bar arch)

Stage (2) 'More somber': bars 8 to 16 (darker colouring with the passage through C minor to a cadence on B♭)

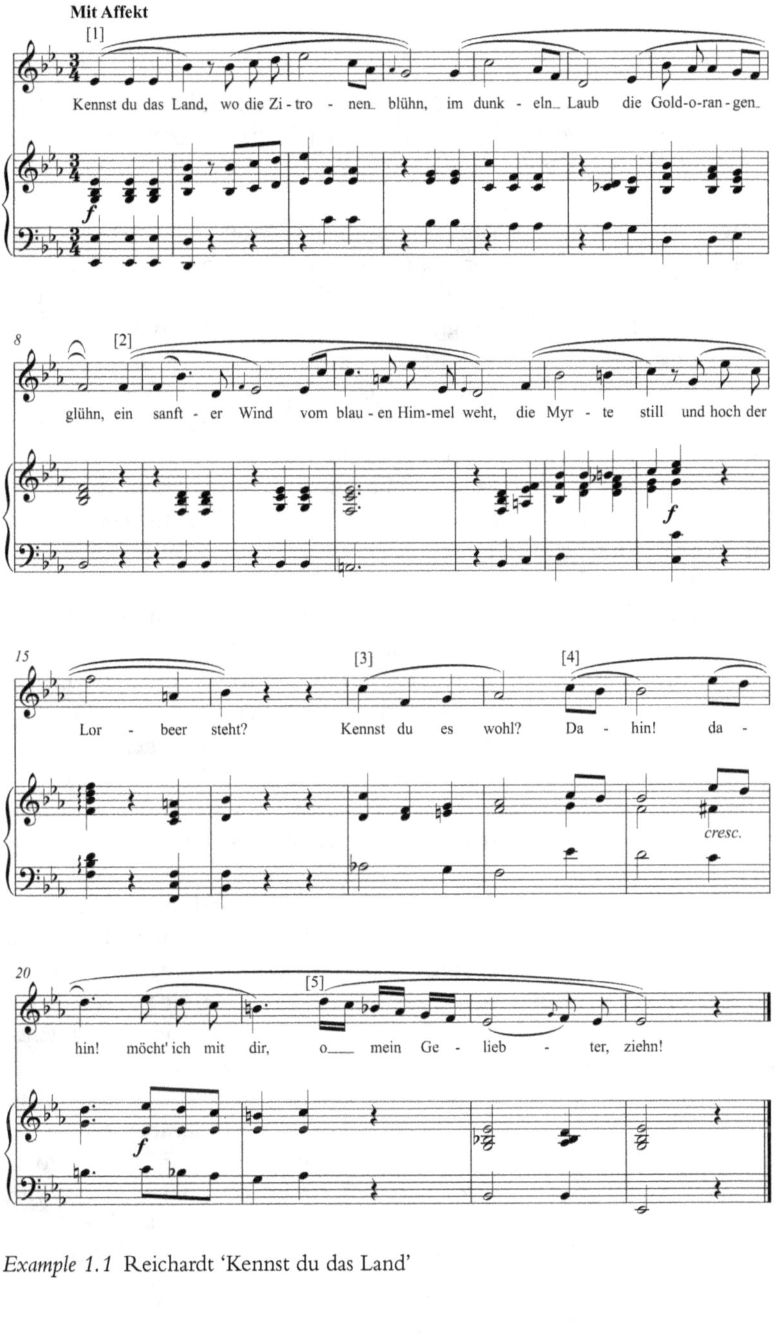

Example 1.1 Reichardt 'Kennst du das Land'

Stage (3) 'Weightiness and mystery': bars 17 to 18 (slowing to a chorale-
like phrase)

Stage (4) 'Suffused with longing': bars 18 to 21 (breaking into more
urgent one-bar phrases)

Stage (5) 'Entreating and urging' or 'pressing and full of promise': bars
21 to 23 (cadential flourish which sweeps the previous one-bar
phrases into a bigger arch)

Viewed in this way, Reichardt's setting comes across as a series of performance hints, pieced together as an accompaniment to the act of reading.
The reader is left to imagine the sound of the simple musical core that
might underlie the rather exaggerated flourishes on the page.

Although Reichardt's setting does not solve the mystery of what
Mignon's song would have sounded like, by including music in his first
edition Goethe makes clear that one should approach her as a listener,
not just a reader. When he returns to the Mignon theme in his second
novel *Wilhelm Meisters Wanderjahre* he underlines even more clearly the
difference between relying on the eye and the ear. There he describes the
efforts of a painter

> to copy from Nature the surroundings in which [Mignon] had lived,
> to portray the lovely child in all the surroundings and moments of
> her life, both happy and unhappy, and so to summon her image,
> which lives in all feeling hearts, before the eye.
>
> (Goethe, 1989, 255)

The artist's journey to Italy results in a remarkable painting that elaborates
upon the scene of the third verse of 'Kennst du das Land' in particular:

> Amidst stark mountain scenery the graceful child, dressed as a boy,
> stands shining, surrounded by sheer cliffs, sprayed by waterfalls, in
> the midst of a band difficult to describe. A horrifying, steep, ancient
> chasm was perhaps never decorated by a more charming or significant
> crew. The colourful, gypsy-like company, at once crude and fantasti-
> cal, exotic and ordinary, too casual to inspire fear, too outlandish to
> awaken trust. Sturdy packhorses plod along, now on corduroy roads,
> now on steps hewn out of the rock, loaded with a jumble of baggage.
> From it dangle all the musical instruments which are needed for a
> bewitching concert, and which now and then molest the ear with
> discordant tones. In the midst of all this the dear child, withdrawn
> into herself, without defiance, reluctant but unresisting, led but not

dragged. Who could have failed to enjoy this remarkable, fully executed picture? The grim defile within the rocky mass was powerfully rendered, the series of black gorges cutting through everything, piled together, threatening to bar any exit, were it not that a boldly suspended bridge suggested the possibility of establishing contact with the outside world. With a clever knack for creating an aura of truth, the artist had also indicated the mouth of a cave, which one might imagine as the workshop where Nature produces giant crystals or the den of a brood of fabulous, frightful dragons.

(Goethe, 1989, 255–256)

But the climax of the painter's efforts comes with a different kind of discovery:

Now it happened that the painter found an unusual instrument in one of the palaces, a small lute, powerful, resonant, convenient to play and carry around. He could soon tune the instrument and play it so well, to the great pleasure of those present, that, like a new Orpheus, he softened the heart of the castellan, otherwise a stern, dry man, and gently compelled him to lend the instrument. . . . From then on the water and the shore were enlivened in quite a different manner. Boats and skiffs vied for their company; even barges and ships bound for market lingered in their vicinity. Processions of people followed them along the shore, and wherever they landed, they were at once surrounded by a lighthearted crowd; when they departed, everyone called out blessings, contented yet full of yearning.

(Goethe, 1989, 257)

Locked in the lute seems to be the aural memory of songs, so that 'like a new Orpheus' the painter draws crowds with him and begins to transform Italy into the kind of Arcadian experience Mignon longs for.

Interestingly, Goethe often referred to himself as an 'eye man', in contrast to Herder whom he called the 'ear man' (Schwab, 1965, 32). But clearly the Mignon version of living by the 'ear' is not to be equated straightforwardly with musical skill; Goethe suggests there is a kind of emptying, a kenosis, involved in tuning the present to the past in the way he describes in the scene from *Wanderjahre*. The painter is a musical amateur, a most unlikely 'new Orpheus'. But in a sense that may be why he promises entry to Mignon's 'land'; the physicality of the sound embodied in the musical instrument speaks for him and creates the immediacy of song. Augustine defines song in such a way, as an experience that is always instantaneously present in its sound:

> We do not first begin to utter formless sounds without singing and then adapt or fashion them into the form of a song, as wood or silver is made into a vessel or a chest – such materials do by time precede the form of the things which are made from them; but in singing this is not so. When a song is sung, its sound is heard at the same time, for there is not a formless sound which is afterwards formed into a song. For as soon as it shall have first sounded it passes away, and you will not find anything remaining of it that you can take up and shape. And, therefore, the song is embodied in its own sound, and that sound is the matter of the song.
>
> (St Augustine, 1993, 255)

It is perhaps in this sense that Mignon's 'Kennst du das Land' offers to turn song into a 'land'; the bare sound of the refrain can ensure community, like a Shakespearean 'Hey-nonny-no'. Yet it still has to be approached that way, which is why Goethe was so critical of the distractions added by Beethoven and Spohr. The song has to be heard and experienced through the quality of refrain-ness, and then it can come across as 'simply a song'. Although Beethoven creates a more definite musical refrain in his setting of 'Kennst du das Land' than Reichardt, Goethe felt that he had missed Mignon's 'distinctive mark', the sign of how the song should act instantly upon the ear. In his setting of 'Kennst du das Land', Beethoven makes the poetic refrain coincide with a return to the song's opening rhythmic phrase, but this returning phrase does not act as a summary of the song as a whole. The two-bar phrase, first introduced by the piano in bar 14 and then repeated by the voice, picks up the compression of the song's opening phrase from four to three bars in the repeat of bars 5 to 7. It also summarises the song's tonal shifts up to this point, between the tonic A and the flat submediant F in bar 12. It draws together the features of the song so far, like an aide memoire, but after a pause in bar 17 the ground shifts to an entirely different song style. The solemn tread of the song's opening is replaced by the faster compound rhythms of a *Tanzlied*. The music at this point is highly communal in character, with swinging thirds and sixths to suggest sympathetic resonance and the lilt of the zither. This is refrain music par excellence, except that it occurs without the song to which it should be attached. 'Dahin! Dahin' ('Oh there, oh there') sings an imaginary chorus, but referring to a 'there' which has not actually been sounded (see Example 1.2).

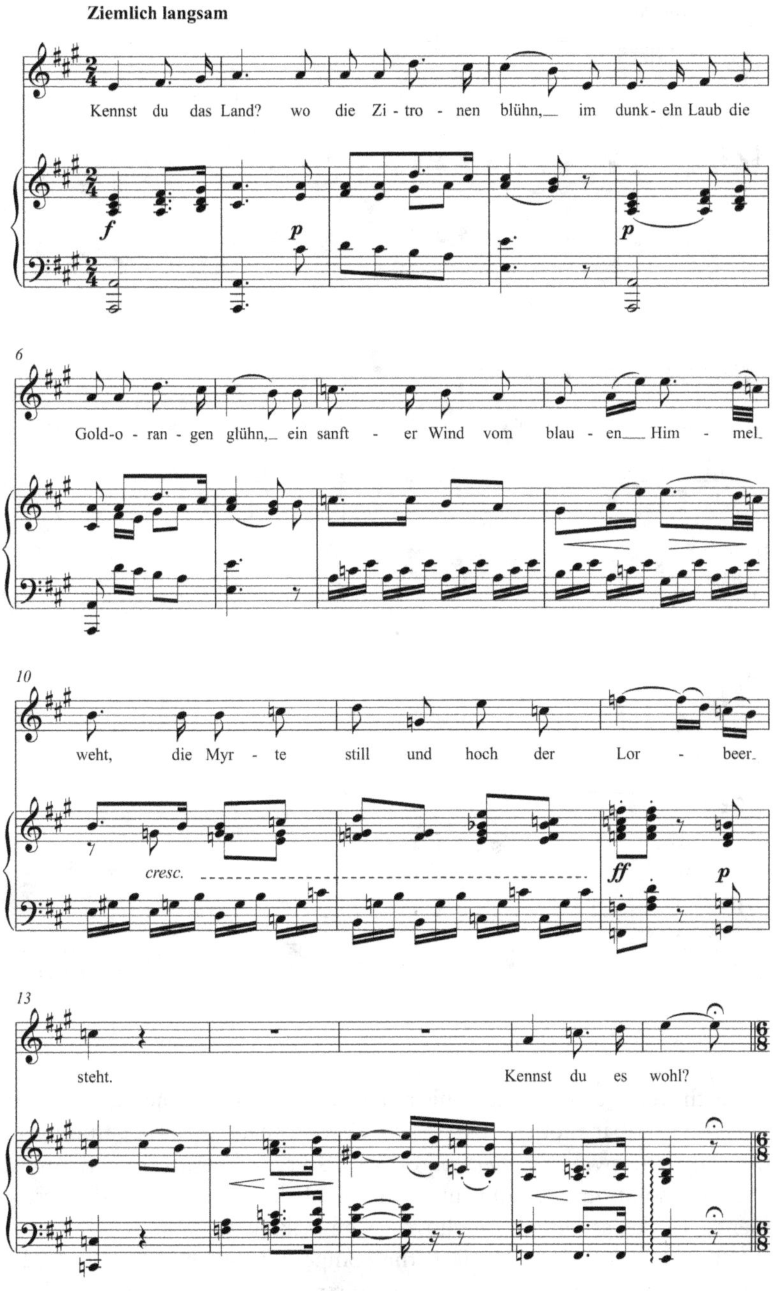

Example 1.2 Beethoven 'Kennst du das Land', bars 1–32

Example 1.2 (Continued)

Beethoven has in fact split his refrain in two around the pause in bar 17. The two-bar motif of bars 14 to 17 looks back to the beginning of the song, the swinging *Tanzlied* of bar 18 urges forwards to a different style of resolution; past and future are divided. Goethe called this treatment aria-like, as though Beethoven were making Mignon switch from a 'cavatina' to a 'cabaletta'. In fact, the composer's treatment is more radical still because the alternation of tempo, metre and style is repeated for each of the song's three verses. The setting is in one sense still strophic, but the strophe is broken in two at the point of refrain. In Reichardt's setting the steady unfolding of two, four and eight-bar phrases keeps the notion of one magnified breath through the first 16 bars of the song (see the phrasing added to Example 1.1). The rests in bar 16 indicate the turning point at the moment of refrain and the beginning of an exhalation over the next seven bars. The ebbing of the breath is indicated by the splitting of 'Dahin! dahin! Möcht' ich mit dir' into one-bar figures, before the steadying flourish of the two-bar closure. The singleness of the song's melodic arch is thus relayed through the implied performance of the breath. Even though Reichardt's music lacks immediate qualities of tunefulness, it retains the equation of strophe with breath and with a single impulse as typifies lyric song. Beethoven, by contrast, keeps the notion of a single breath only up to the cadence in the thirteenth bar of each strophe; then the piano intervenes to sound the moment of refrain as though the voice were faltering. The pause at the end of the singer's echo of the piano's phrase can even be taken as dying into silence, as indicated by the rests in the piano part at this point. Her following 'Dahin! dahin!' makes its impact as an entirely new breath, whether snatched or coming from a deeper intake of air. It is as though Beethoven were encouraging the listener to watch the drama of Mignon's breath rather than to join in with her, to watch as would be characteristic of experiencing an operatic mode of address. The timing of the breath for 'Dahin!' cannot be predicted from what has gone before, even with the threefold repetition, because it comes from a different impulse than the hymn-like style of the opening. In fact the performance of the repetition creates further tensions as the listener waits to see how the moment of pausing will impact upon the contrasts of each verse.

For Goethe, watching Mignon rather than joining in with her means that she is not present in the sense that he wishes, nor is her 'land'. The verdict 'Mignon would not have sung that' is highly significant. Goethe implies Beethoven is handing over Mignon's voice to a trained operatic singer rather than allowing a more natural voice to emerge. Mignon's 'land' invokes communality, and in some sense her song should be capable of being sung by anyone. Goethe makes clear that her skills as a singer are to be deployed to lessen the distance between herself and her listener, as reflecting the ideals of the *Im Volkston* movement. For the poet Achim von Arnim, in his essay 'On Folk Songs', these ideals are realised most closely in the songs of Johann Abraham Peter Schulz, from which emanates a true tone 'comparable to that kind of laughter which comes from the bottom of one's heart' (Siegel, 1983, 194). For all Goethe's criticisms of him, Beethoven had firsthand experience of such song practices through his early years as a student of Christian Gottlob Neefe, and there are signs that he was not immune to Mignon's evocation of a child-like appeal for sympathy. He employs a distinctly different, non-operatic vocal style for his setting of the Mignon lyric, 'Nur wer die Sehnsucht kennt', a lyric which he turned to in 1807 two years before 'Kennst du das Land'. He produced four different settings of this lyric and wrote over the manuscript 'I didn't have time to produce *one good one*, so here are several attempts' (Reid, 2007, 250). His attempts are marked by extreme simplicity and compression, aspects that are relatively rare in Beethoven's song-writing. It is as though in honour of Mignon the composer were minded to strip his compositional means to the bare minimum, even though he could not prevent a kind of creative overspill from one version to the next.

Comparing Beethoven's first two settings of 'Nur wer die Sehnsucht kennt', the compositional overflow from one song to the next is imme-diately clear, to the extent that the second song begins with the spe-cific melodic shape of the third bar of the first setting (see Examples 1.3 and 1.4). Yet interestingly enough, the second song 'composes out' the first song by offering a further compression of melody rather than an expansion. In contrast to the twisting rise and falls of the first song's open-ing phrase, the second song offers in essence one stark descent, from melodic dominant to tonic. The pause on A, the supertonic, at the close of the phrase only delays the inevitable, as traced in the descent of the last four bars. Given that Beethoven construes Goethe's single poetic strophe as a repeat of one 11-bar musical statement, the same descent is heard four times in quick succession. The rising profile of bars 5 to 7 is like the briefest of links, preparing for the further descent. It would be hard to find a song more concentrated on a single melodic profile, more focused on offering a 'distinctive mark', to use Goethe's phrase. The 'distinctive mark' of Mignon's poem in this instance is not so much a refrain as the constant repetition of certain rhyming syllables, as with the obsessive sounds of 'de', 'nt' and 'te' which indicate the groans issuing deep from her insides:

> Nur wer die Sehnsucht kennt,
> Weiss, was ich leide!
> Allein und abgetrennt
> Von aller Freude,
> Seh' ich ans Firmament
> Nach jener Seite.
> Ach! Der mich liebt und kennt
> Ist in der Weite.
> Es schwindelt mir, es brennt

Example 1.3 Beethoven 'Nur wer die Sehnsucht kennt' (first version)

Mein Eingeweide.
Nur wer die Sehnsucht kennt,
Weiss, was ich leide!
> (Goethe, 1986, 87)

[Only they know my pain
Who know my yearning!
Parted and lone again,
All joy unlearning,
I scan all heaven's demesne

Example 1.4 Beethoven 'Nur wer die Sehnsucht kennt' (second version)

For any turning.
Ah, but my love and swain –
Far he's sojourning.
Hot is my spinning brain,
My insides burning.
Only they know my pain
Who know my yearning!]
(Goethe, 1995, 142–143)

The repeated 'ei' is like the sound of physical keening, as summed up most powerfully in 'Eingeweide', the word for 'insides'. The poem seems to collapse inwards, and yet in the novel Goethe indicates that this lyric is sung as a duet between Mignon and the Harper. The groans of inner pain are offered as a communal tune or sing-song, as Beethoven implies in his second setting through the rhythmic ease of his swinging 6/8 metre. The exaggeratedly simple accompaniment suggests the strumming of a lute, like the one found by the artist in *Wilhelm Meisters Wanderjahre*.

In a sense it is not surprising that Beethoven dubbed such a song as not a proper setting. There is much about it that seems barely formed – the emptiness and low register of the piano textures, the 'tum-ti-tum' sequential padding in the melody's central phrase. As in an internalised hum, the patterns of melody keep circling back to the same point. The song's end blurs into the beginning, except that the piano's last-minute insertion of an F# in bar 7 marks a specific pull back. At the moment where the voice rests on the last quaver of bar 7, the piano insinuates the need for return, as though the singer's breath were collapsing and incapable of sustaining a wider melodic arch. The swift insertion of the F#, which redirects the song back to the tonic G minor from the relative B♭ major, offers a moment of drama, though one which could be missed were it not an echo of the similar moment of melodic and tonal return in bar 7 of Beethoven's first setting. Here the voice's chromatic descent dramatises the collapse of the breath in a much more explicit fashion; the unexpected extension of the final syllable of 'Freude' or 'Eingeweide' reveals a declamatory impulse that threatens to contradict the evenness of the song's melodic style. At the moment of return the panting rhythms of the piano accompaniment infect the vocal part to suggest an inherent fragility in the rise and fall of the song's melodic profile.

In both of these settings Beethoven uses the melodic repetition to reinforce the triumph of lyricism over any moments of potential drama; each remains an essentially simple song. Yet more significantly still, Beethoven uses the second song to reinforce the melodic emphasis of the first, so that its simplicity becomes pointedly didactic. Beethoven seeks to match Mignon's extreme poetic introspection with the closing three bars of the second setting, where her melody is presented as a circular rocking around two interlocking thirds, C-A and B♭-G. The vertical and horizontal, melodic and tonal dimensions of the song are brought to rest in a single interval, the B♭-G with which the voice closes. This dying fall, B♭-G, is picked up as the starting point for the circling melodic arches of the third song, except that the interval is now presented vertically within the context of an E♭ triad. In this third setting each melodic phrase pulls away from and then back towards the harmonic and melodic nexus of

B♭–G–E♭. The pull back is highlighted by the interlude in bar 7 and by the postlude, but it also appears within the setting's opening phrase so that the whole song is in a sense completed by its third bar:

Example 1.5 Beethoven 'Nur wer die Sehnsucht kennt' (third version)

In this third song Beethoven indicates how Mignon's lyric contracts as it expands with the gracious arches of melody being drawn back to one point of musical closure; just as poetically, Mignon uses alliteration and assonance to link the wideness of the 'Firmament' to the immediate burning of her 'Eingeweide'. The song is shown to turn on a single space-time axis, as the intervallic thirds are presented as giving both vertical padding and horizontal direction. Such dancing up and down on one spot is summed up by the piano interlude in bar 7. What might seem like a conventional link, with repeated B♭s preparing for the moment of melodic and harmonic return in bar 8, is highlighted by internal voice-leading as being simultaneously the rediscovery of the crucial intervallic pairing of B♭ with G. The movements to and from G at this point create a stasis, a blurring of here and there. In the postlude G is both an arrival, in the resolution from A♭ to G in the tenor register on the second beat of bar 11, and a departure-point in the top part's G dissonance within the dominant thirteenth on the first beat.

In the third setting of 'Nur wer die Sehnsucht kennt' the role of the piano is crucial in highlighting the exchange between melodic and harmonic parameters. This is definitely a keyboard song, in contrast to the evocation of a voice and lute combination in the first two settings. However, when hearing the third song in the context of the previous two, its most important stylistic aspect becomes the transformation of time into space in a way that captures the instantaneous qualities of song. In highlighting the impact of single moments Beethoven also allows the heightened charge of performance to be composed into the fabric of the song. The piano's postlude of bars 10 to 11 offers completion – as marked by the finishing touch of the emphatic low E♭ – as well as an echo of what has just been sung from bars 9 to 10. It hovers between future and past in a way that sums up what happens in performance, as well as offering potential to performers. Since Beethoven's again splits Goethe's strophe into two repeated 11-bar statements, the listener has the opportunity to savour what happens to the piano's closing cadence on repeat. Beethoven uses the musical repetition to stoke listeners' expectation as the pianist is left to make the summary of the song – the song as it was, or as it now becomes.

Mignon's repeat of the first two lines of 'Nur wer die Sehnsucht kennt' as the last two lines of her poem sets up just such a sense of uncertainty. The choice between hearing these lines as returning or concluding suggests that one approaches them through time. But given the degree of assonance and alliteration that occurs throughout the poem, one might hear the sound of the opening lines as continually sustained, as a powerful evocation of timelessness. Nothing happens except the one groan of longing. The travelling implied by references to the 'Firmament' and 'in der Weite' happens through distances of space, not time. Time is lost in the notion of dizziness, 'Es schwindelt mir', and of gazing into the depths – whether internal or external. The poem is not just 'an echo' of the 'state of dreamy longing' that Wilhelm was feeling (Goethe, 1995,

142); as it probes the effect of such longing the transitory becomes a definite mode of processing experience. In the manner of its conclusion, with the repeat of its opening, the poem shows how it becomes what it is: lyric song. And it is just such self-awareness that Beethoven reflects with the closing cadence of his third setting of 'Nur wer die Sehnsucht kennt'. In that moment the song reveals its process of becoming song, lyric song in particular.

With his manner of approaching 'Nur wer die Sehnsucht kennt', one might say Beethoven shows an essential understanding of what the appellation 'lyric' implies. Georg Lukács believes that it is a definition of the lyric that single moments become constitutive and form-determining:

> Only in lyric poetry do these direct sudden flashes of the substance become like lost original manuscripts suddenly made legible.
>
> (Lukács, 1971, 62)

Lukács sees such moments as all-consuming:

> In lyric poetry, only the great moment exists, the moment at which the meaningful unity of nature and soul or their meaningful divorce, the necessary and affirmed loneliness of the soul becomes eternal. At the lyrical moment the purest interiority of the soul, set apart from duration without choice, lifted above the obscurely-determined multiplicity of things, solidifies into substance.
>
> (Lukács, 1971, 62)

Lukács's reference to 'the purest interiority of soul' immediately brings Mignon's 'Nur wer die Sehnsucht kennt' to mind. His notion of avoiding the 'obscurely-determined multiplicity of things' also chimes in with Goethe's distrust of complication in the lyric. If in lyric poetry the substance reveals itself 'in sudden flashes', then an 11-year-old child might be held up as the perfect lyricist. Such childlike-ness does not seem to have come easily to Beethoven. Though he showed his sympathy with the challenge of singing Mignon in his 'Nur wer die Sehnsucht kennt' settings, he dismissed his achievements by saying he had failed to create 'one good one'. Something was clearly left incomplete in his mind, even with the beautifully turned melodic process of his third setting.

Beethoven's dismissive comment becomes even more surprising as one turns to his fourth setting of 'Nur wer die Sehnsucht kennt'. This song suggests the composer expending effort to create a composite song from aspects of the previous three settings. The key and metre immediately refer to the second song, though the melodic style of the opening phrase is more reminiscent of the rise and falls of the first song, whilst the piano echo from bar 4 to 5, with its summary of the predominant B♭–G interval, refers back to the cadential figure of the third setting. Thus, even within its opening statement, the song brings together key aspects of all three previous settings:

Example 1.6 Beethoven 'Nur wer die Sehnsucht kennt' (fourth version)

Example 1.6 (Continued)

Beethoven continues to play with memories of all of his three other settings; he even creates a kind of layered outcome as he develops each song's ingredients. The first answer to the song's opening statement, from bars 5 to 11, takes up the loosely circling sequences from the central phrase of the second song. This is followed by a statement from bar 13 to 17 that follows the key (E♭) and melodic shapes of the third song, a reference that is underlined by a piano link in bar 12 that directly echoes bar 7 of the third setting. Bars 17 to 20 follow closely bars 5 to 7 of the first setting, complete with the voice's faltering chromatic descent from D back to B♭ at the end of the phrase. The connections are skillfully made, and it would be possible to sing this song as a separate, more developmental response to Mignon's longing. Given that Beethoven does not set up a large-scale repeat in this setting, unlike in the other three, there are opportunities for word-painting that give an extra vividness. The declamatory approach to 'allein und abgetrennt' in bars 5 to 7, and to 'es schwindelt mir' from bar 17, adds urgency to the contrasts of melodic style. However, it would be inaccurate to view this song as entirely through-composed. The return to the opening phrase from bars 21 to 24 is still the highlight of the setting, and the subsequent echoes from voice and piano are clearly designed to draw the melody back to a single point, the B♭-G interval as heard on the first beat of the final bar. For all its layering of contrasts, the song ends with a single point of intervallic closure in the manner of the second and third settings.

With the overall predominance of the B♭-G interval across his four versions of 'Nur wer die Sehnsucht kennt', Beethoven might be heard as offering a kind of *Ur*-setting. When he said he did not have time to complete 'one good song', the assumption is that he meant to write a more fully composed setting. Yet, given the persistent references to melodic compactness, Beethoven may have been wishing for more time to empty himself of his usual compositional impulses and find a different way of dealing with musical memory. Seen in this light the extreme simplicity of some of Beethoven's late songs, as discussed in Chapter 4, might be seen as his continuing response to the challenge of singing Mignon, though from a point of even greater compositional subtlety. The experiment of the 'Nur wer die Sehnsucht kennt' settings certainly leaves tantalising question marks over the nature of Beethoven's response to Goethe's Mignon. There is no complete Mignon offered here, but there are signs that the composer still wished to embrace her way of singing from a point of absolute interiority. The same might be said of his 'Kennst du das Land' setting, even though here Beethoven offers a provocatively divided Mignon. Goethe says that music should always relate to one of two poles, either the 'numinous nature of church music' or the 'cheerfulness and playfulness of folk melodies'; any mixture of chorale and dance is confusing (Goethe, 1998, 64). In his 'Kennst du das Land', Beethoven creates a setting that refers to each pole in turn, as though two songs are to be held in the head simultaneously. For Goethe such complication reflects the state of Beethoven's mind rather than Mignon's, but something about Beethoven's way of building memory in the song could still be said to probe Mignon's efforts to find a 'land' in song. Although it contrasts so markedly in style with the opening of the song, the section that emerges in bar 18 soon reveals itself as a series of elaborations on the single D-C# melodic inflection with which the *Tanzlied* starts. This anacrustic impulse becomes the focus of repetition and even of closure, as the following sequence reduces into smaller and smaller circles. What seemed like expansion turns into contraction, even to the single point of an appoggiatura over the tonic triad in bar 30 (see Example 1.2). The *Tanzlied* dwindles into nothing, or more significantly the D-C# is left exposed for an aural connection with the melodic descent, D-C#-B, that marks the imperfect cadences in bars 4 and 7 of the song's opening section. Harmonically these imperfect cadences are picked up in the refrain motif of bars 14–15. But more significantly perhaps the melodic contraction to a simple D-C# at the 'Geschwinder' prompts the memory of the imperfect cadences to be now linked to a perfect cadence on the tonic. The basic sound of Mignon's song is heard to carry through and resolve even while the style of the song fractures. One might say that in the essential sound of her song Mignon finds Arcadia, even though from an external stylistic viewpoint her music appears broken by exile.

Goethe was clearly not content to entertain such compositional niceties in the interpretation of Mignon's lyrics. But Herder, in many ways the inspiration for the association of Mignon's singing with land, gives eloquent expression to the double experience of communion and exile that comes with memories of Arcadia. In the preface to his 1779 collection of 'Volkslieder', Herder writes (Herder, 1885, 316):

> O that I might succeed in translating these most noble folksongs into our language, so that some of what they are might linger on. Homer, Hesiod, Orpheus, I see your shadows there in front of me among the crowd on the island of the blessed and I hear the echoes of your songs; but here on my land and in my language I lack the ship that can take me to you. On the journey the waves of the sea silence the harps and the wind blows your songs back to where, in endless dances and feasts under Amaranthian arbours they will never die away.
>
> (Author's translation)

For Herder, the act of translation involves dealing with echoes from a land that is simultaneously there and not there. Mignon is thus dealing with shadows or can even be construed as a shadow herself – like Homer, Hesiod and Orpheus. It might be unfair to suggest that Beethoven grasps the elusive nature of Mignon better than Goethe himself, but in insisting on his own view of her powers of memory-making, he pays them a meaningful tribute. For creating a 'land' out of memory suggests offering an experience that can transcend any origins and become truly communal – provided receivers respond to the challenge of seeking to listen and to join in.

References

Byrne, Lorraine (ed.). *Goethe: Musical Poet, Musical Catalyst*. Dublin: Carysfort Press, 2004.

Eckermann, Johann Peter. *Conversations with Goethe*, ed. J.K. Moorhead, tr. John Oxenford. London: Dent, 1970.

Goethe, Johann Wolfgang von. *Conversations and Encounters*, ed. and tr. David Luke and Robert Pick. London: Oswald Wolff, 1966.

Goethe, Johann Wolfgang von. *Italian Journey*, tr. W.H. Auden and Elizabeth Mayer. Harmondsworth: Penguin Books, 1982.

Goethe, Johann Wolfgang von. *Selected Verse*, ed. David Luke. Harmondsworth: Penguin Books, 1986.

Goethe, Johann Wolfgang von. *Wilhelm Meister's Journeyman Years or the Renunciants*, ed. Jane K. Brown, tr. Krishna Winston. Princeton, NJ: Princeton University Press, 1989.

Goethe, Johann Wolfgang von. *Selected Poems*, ed. Christopher Middleton. Princeton, NJ: Princeton University Press, 1994.

Goethe, Johann Wolfgang von. *Wilhelm Meister's Apprenticeship*, ed. and tr. Eric A. Blackall. Princeton, NJ: Princeton University Press, 1995.

Goethe, Johann Wolfgang von. *Maxims and Reflections*, ed. Peter Hutchinson, tr. Elisabeth Stopp. Harmondsworth: Penguin Books, 1998.

Grillparzer, Franz. *Sämtliche Werke*. Volume 2, ed. Peter Frank and Karl Pörnbacher. Munich, Germany: Carl Hanser, 1964.

Hamburger, Michael (ed.). *Beethoven: Letters, Journals and Conversations*. London: Thames and Hudson, 1951.

Herder, Johann Gottfried. *Sämtliche Werke*. Volume 25, ed. Berhard Suphan. Berlin, Germany: Weidmann, 1885.

Jander, Owen. 'Let Your Deafness No Longer Be a Secret – Even in Art': Self-Portraiture and the Third Movement of the C Minor Symphony. *Beethoven Forum* 8 (1), 2008: 25–70.

Lukács, Georg. *The Theory of the Novel*, tr. Anna Bostock. London: Merlin Press, 1971.

Moser, Hans Joachim. *Goethe und die Musik*. Leipzig, Germany: Peters, 1949.

Němec, Zdeněk. *Vlastní Životopis V.J. Tomáška*. Prague: Topičova edice v Praze, 1941.

New International Version of the Bible. London: Hodder and Stoughton, 2011.

Reichardt, Johann Friedrich. *Goethes Lieder, Oden, Balladen und Romanzen mit Musik*, ed. Hermann Wetzel. Berlin, Germany: Verlagsanstalt Hymnophon, n.d.

Reid, Paul. *The Beethoven Song Companion*. Manchester: Manchester University Press, 2007.

Schopenhauer, Arthur. *The World as Will and Representation*. Volume 2, tr. E.F.J. Payne. New York: Dover Publications, 1958.

Schwab, Heinrich W. *Sangbarkeit, Popularität und Kunstlied: Studien zu Lied und Liedästhetik der mittleren Goethezeit 1770–1814*. Regensburg: Gustav Bosse, 1965.

Siegel, Linda (ed. and tr.). *Music in German Romantic Literature*. Novato, CA: Elra Publications, 1983.

St Augustine. *Confessions*, ed. Justin Lovill, tr. J.G. Pilkington. London: Folio Society, 1993.

Sternfeld, Frederick. *Goethe and Music: A List of Parodies*. New York: New York Public Library, 1954.

2   To a distant beloved

Beethoven's tribute to strophic song

Mignon's call 'Do you know the land' echoes Herder's vision of poetry as the 'land of the soul' (Chamberlain, 1992, 168). With his following quote from Virgil's *Aeneid*, *'tendimus in Arcadium, tendimus'* (we are making our way to Arcadia), Herder makes clear that such a land must be sought in community. Like Schumann he believes all lyricists, whether musicians or poets, draw from a common source. As Schumann puts it in his essay 'On the Inner Relationship of Poetry and Music':

> Do you think that a Schiller, a Goethe, a Klopstock and the whole group of splendid singers of the German people did not derive their inspiration for their songs from the same holy fountain which brought forth the harmonies of a Mozart, a Haydn or a Hummel.
>
> (Siegel, 1983, 266–267)

Schumann imagines poetry and music walking 'hand-in-hand down their heavenly path' (Siegel, 1983, 265). Yet the example of Beethoven's 'Kennst du das Land' suggests a composer struggling to find a lyric voice that can both respond to words and outstrip their meanings. There was a competitive edge to Beethoven's song-writing that has been recognised by Jack Stein:

> From Beethoven and Schubert on the poem became, in a sense, embattled, by virtue of the fact that music had developed more precise and also more powerful means of extending poetic ideas into its own more abstract sphere.
>
> (Stein, 1971, 17)

Stein imparts a kind of stark inevitability to such developments, as though music wrests power from poetry as part of a progression in style and language. However, Beethoven's response to the figure of Mignon is highly nuanced, with different possibilities being offered to the receptive listener. As with his four settings of Mignon's 'Wer nur die Sehnsucht kennt', Beethoven plays with various kinds of musical repetition – at different levels of detail – so that the listener has to decide where to pitch the relationship of poetic and musical identities. 'Kennst du das Land' is a song in flux, waiting for performers – and listeners – to make sense of its contrasts and pauses, just as they have to assemble a response to 'Wer nur die Sehnsucht kennt' from Beethoven's multiple versions.

Barry Cooper believes it is Beethoven, not Schubert, who should truly be credited with the creation of the German Romantic Lied (Cooper, 1996, 262). If Beethoven's 'Kennst du das Land' is taken as an early landmark, then it establishes the genre as a place of speculation about musical and poetic boundaries. Even the usual generic markers that distinguish lyric from dramatic song, 'Lied' from 'Gesang', become blurred. As set out by commentators such as Heinrich W. Schwab, the 'Lied' is characterised by strophic structures, by the circular repetitions of a musical melody to align with poetic repetitions of metre, line and stanza. The 'Gesang' is conceived as a through-composed structure, characterised by developmental contrast and the desire to find a quasi-dramatic outcome (Schwab, 1965, 51–56). As should be clear from the discussions in Chapter 1, Beethoven's 'Kennst du das land' can be heard to belong in either category. Even the collection of 'Wer nur die Sehnsucht kennt' settings can be viewed in two ways; either the collection can be seen to foreground repetitive strophic melodies for their own sake, or it can seem to use them to highlight the more developed textures of the fourth and final setting. It is common for composers to vary their musical treatment – moving between the strophic and through-composed – according to the particular poem and their way of reading it, but not to create such variance or flux within the approach to the same poem. It is as though Beethoven does not hear a poem generically, or rather that he responds to it from some point of abstraction that allows him to play with different styles of setting. As in the quotation above, Jack Stein sees a tendency to abstraction as a sign of composers reverting to their own musical sphere. But in poetic terms abstraction might mean holding onto the essential sense of the poet's 'I sing' irrespective of the forms or styles in which it appears. It might mean agreeing with Herder that lyric should be taken as referring to a mode of address, as an 'energy' or 'force', rather than as a generic type (Chamberlain, 1992, 131).

In casting the lyric in this light Herder was setting himself up against the rage for definition of his time. Lessing was the immediate butt of Herder's criticism. But Schiller and Goethe carried on the urge to find terms for the indefinable, one of the most famous examples being Schiller's distinction between categories of 'naïve' and 'sentimental' poetry. It is tempting to align these poetic categories with the musical ones of 'Lied' and 'Gesang' already noted. Schiller's description of the 'naïve' poet's method of working accords well with the notion of immediate melodic fulfilment enshrined in strophic forms:

> All the powers of his humanity are brought to bear in a single moment, he needs nothing, he is a whole in himself.
>
> (Schiller, 1993, 75, author's translation)

The 'sentimental' poet, by contrast, is driven to develop his feelings to create a whole, as befits the notion of a 'Gesang':

> Here he feels only an urgent impulse, to create the harmony in himself, as he truly experiences it, to make a whole out of himself, to bring his humanity to its completest expression. Where his spirit is all in movement, stirred up, swaying between conflicting feelings, there it is at peace, joyful, at one with itself and entirely satisfied.
>
> (Author's translation)

Giving the distinction in its baldest terms, Schiller says that whilst the sentimental poet seeks nature, the naïve poet *is* nature (Schiller, 1993, 30). The implication is that a poet, a poem, a song will be driven to follow a particular path, channelled by a particular character that determines stylistic choices and responses. Beethoven's character is usually associated with the category of the 'sentimental'; the poet Ludwig Tieck, for one, comments on the striking 'restlessness' of his songs (Siegel, 1983, 113). Having established such an association, Schiller would make this the foil for any contrasts, as when he discussed Goethe's *Werther* as an example of a 'naïve' poet dealing with a 'sentimental' subject (Schiller, 1993, 58). It was not that Schiller necessarily wished to give aesthetic preeminence to one category or the other; this is confirmed by his identifying Goethe as 'naïve' and a poet of such weight as Milton as 'sentimental' (Schiller, 1993, 72). The crucial aspect was that there should remain a distinction, a way of making sense of the contradictions that often came with the lyric. For example, Herder's advocacy of Ossian as lyricist suggested mixing up personal and public forms of communication, turning the 'I sing' of Pindar or Homer into a communal 'sing-song'. For Schiller, and Goethe, the worst results of this confusion were to be seen in the poetry of Gottfried August Bürger, whom Schiller accused of dropping down to the level of the people rather than drawing them to himself (Schiller, 1968, 682;

Chamberlain, 1992, 267). Underlying Bürger's poetry was indeed a defiance of any aspiration to write 'higher lyric poetry', or to acknowledge any such aesthetic distinctions. In his essay 'Outpourings from the Heart on Folk Poetry', he writes:

> Pull out the magic wand of the natural epos! Set it all in swarming tumult! Chase it before the eyes of the imagination! Let fly the golden arrows! Truly! Then shall things go differently from the way they have until now! I promise anyone who achieves this that his song will enrapture the refined sage just as much as the rude forest dweller, the lady at her dressing table as much as the daughter of nature at her spinning wheel and at the laundry. Let this be the real ultimate height of poetry.
>
> (Chamberlain, 1992, 254–255)

Bürger is now mostly remembered for his folk-inspired ballads. He might best be treated as a footnote to Goethe and Schiller, were it not that Beethoven set some of his lyric poems and seems to have found a crucial point of song identity through him. There is some dispute whether Bürger might not have been the poet of *Schilderung eines Mädchens*, the first song attributed to Beethoven (Stoljar, 1985, 137; Reid, 2007, 244–245). It is certainly true that the composer made three Bürger settings in the early years of his move to Vienna, even though, according to Douglas Johnson, he was then seeking to impress the Viennese public with his command of the more sophisticated keyboard song (Johnson, 1982, 22–24). Bürger's poetry speaks of Beethoven's North German beginnings; as Paul Reid says, he was probably introduced to it by his Bonn teacher, Neefe, an advocate of the *Im Volkston* style of song-writing (Reid, 2007, 276). This style was inspired by the Göttingen Hainbund, a group of poets with whom Bürger was closely associated. Yet each of these three settings gives a very different view of how Beethoven was processing the influences of his early years. The most famous of the three settings involves a pairing of two Bürger poems, *Seufzer eines Ungeliebten* and *Gegenliebe*, the first poem being transformed into an operatic cavatina, complete with introductory recitative. The second song in the pairing makes reference to a folk-like style, though more in the manner of Papageno in *Zauberflöte* than an evocation of what an entirely untrained singer might actually sing. There is a clear distinction between *Gegenliebe* and Beethoven's setting of Bürger's *Das Blümchen Wunderhold*, which, though it probably comes from the same early-Vienna period, makes minimal use of instrumental means and seems designed to mimic a simple ditty as much as possible. With this song it is as if the composer wished to pay direct tribute to Bürger's ideal of art keeping close to nature:

> My ear has often listened at dusk to the magic sound of ballads and popular songs, beneath the linden trees in a village, at the laundry, and in spinning rooms. Rarely has a little ditty, as they call it, been too nonsensical and absurd not to have offered at least something, if only a brush stroke of magically rusty coloration, which edified me poetically.
>
> (Chamberlain, 1992, 255)

There is a challenging sense of longing in Bürger's evocation of rural scenes; he believes the poet or composer needs to convey a touch of 'magic' if the song is to edify as it should. In his *Wunderhold* poem, the poet speaks of the charming flower of modesty ('Bescheidenheit') with increasing fervour, so that from delighting the eye like 'rays of evening sunshine' it comes to transform every aspect of mind and sense:

> Es blüht ein Blümchen irgend wo
> In einem stillen Thal.
> Das schmeichelt Aug' und Herz so froh,
> Wie Abendsonnenstrahl.
> Das ist viel köstlicher, als Gold,
> Als Perl' und Diamant.
> Drum wird es 'Blümchen Wunderhold'
> Mit gutem Fug genannt.
>
> Wohl sänge sich ein langes Lied
> Von meines Blümchens Kraft:
> Wie es am Leib und am Gemüt
> So hohe Wunder schafft.
> Was kein geheimes Elixier
> Dir sonst gewähren kann,
> Das leistet traun! mein Blümchen dir.
> Man säh' es ihm nicht an.
>
> (Bürger, 1789, 263)

> [A little flower blossoms
> Somewhere in a quiet valley.
> It brings joy to eye and heart
> Like rays of evening sunshine.

It is more precious than gold,
Than pearls and diamonds.
Thus it is called with good reason
'The flower beyond price'.

It would be good to sing a lengthy song
Of the effect of my little flower:
Of how it works wonders
For body and soul.
What no secret elixir
Can ever grant you,
Believe me, my flower can do;
Though one would not think to look at it.]
(Author's translation)

These two verses are followed by ten more in Bürger's original. The song is indeed 'lengthy', though in the final verse the poet says 'the longest song will never grasp' what is truly at stake:

O was des Blümchens Wunderkraft
Am Leib' und am Gemüt
Ihr, meiner Holdin, einst verschafft,
Faßt nicht das längste Lied! –
Weil's mehr, als Seide, Perl' und Gold
Der Schönheit Zier verleiht,
So nenn' ichs 'Blümchen Wunderhold'
Sonst heißt's – Bescheidenheit.

[Oh, what you once bestowed, my dear one,
Upon my body and soul,
With the flower's wondrous power
The longest song will never grasp! –
Because more than silk, pearls or gold
It gives value to beauty,
So I name it 'the flower beyond price',
Otherwise it is called – modesty.]
(Author's translation)

The key word is 'once'; in verse 10 the poet reveals that the beloved who personifies modesty is now dead. Her flower-like quality has to be invoked through a recital of memory, just as Bürger seeks to remember the sound of songs under the linden tree.

Bürger's theme of flower-like modesty clearly inhibited Beethoven from offering an operatically or instrumentally conceived setting in the manner of *Gegenliebe*. But then the question arises why he wished to make the setting at all, and having made it, to include it as the final song in his Op. 52 collection. As with the 'Nur wer die Sehnsucht kennt' series, it is tempting to see the last song of the series as the summation or reference point for the rest. In which case, the extreme simplicity of Beethoven's *Wunderhold* becomes a measure for, or a comment on, the style of the other seven songs. Looking at the set as a whole, the two songs that most immediately resemble *Wunderhold* are Beethoven's setting of *Urians Reise um die Welt* by the Göttinger Hainbund poet Claudius and the setting of Goethe's *Marmotte*. They share *Wunderhold*'s exaggerated use of musical repetition, the swinging V-I upbeats to encourage communal singing and the limited guitar-like accompaniment style. Yet the Claudius and Goethe settings seem intended as occasional songs, opportunities for a communal sing-song, in the way that *Wunderhold* is not; one can see this from the 'Tutti' marking for the final four bars of the verse in *Urians Reise*, and the constant refrain of 'Avecque la Marmotte' in the Goethe song. In *Wunderhold*, by contrast, the *sempre piano* instruction and the delicate articulation invite those present to listen rather than raucously join in. Also the V-I 'all together now' signal occurs with the second phrase of the song, not the first. The first phrase creeps in over a melodic dominant, pitched uncomfortably at a break in the voice and without harmonic support. One phrase floats, the second phrase comes to ground. But with the constant alternation of the two, within the single verse and across the repetition of verses, the sense of tiptoeing around what should be a simple *Tanzlied* continues. Indeed the tempo marking, *Andante*, is slightly slower than what one might expect from the song's basic style; what should skip seems to have become a walk (see Example 2.1).

Beethoven thus hints at a possible *espressivo* rendering of *Wunderhold* that links it to his other Bürger setting from the Op. 52 collection, *Mollys Abschied*, a setting which he marks *Adagio con espressione*. The Molly of this poem is known to be the same person as the personification of modesty in *Wunderhold*, so a connection would be expected. However, apart from the implied tenderness of both, the songs seem to belong in different stylistic worlds. In Bürger's terminology the laundry maid of *Wunderhold* has been replaced by a lady, in the sense that *Mollys Abschied* is a harmonically and texturally developed keyboard song; North-German sensibilities have been replaced by Viennese ones. A sonata–influenced instrumental style is similarly apparent in two other songs from the Op. 52 collection, in the setting of Lessing's *Die Liebe* and of Goethe's *Mailied*.

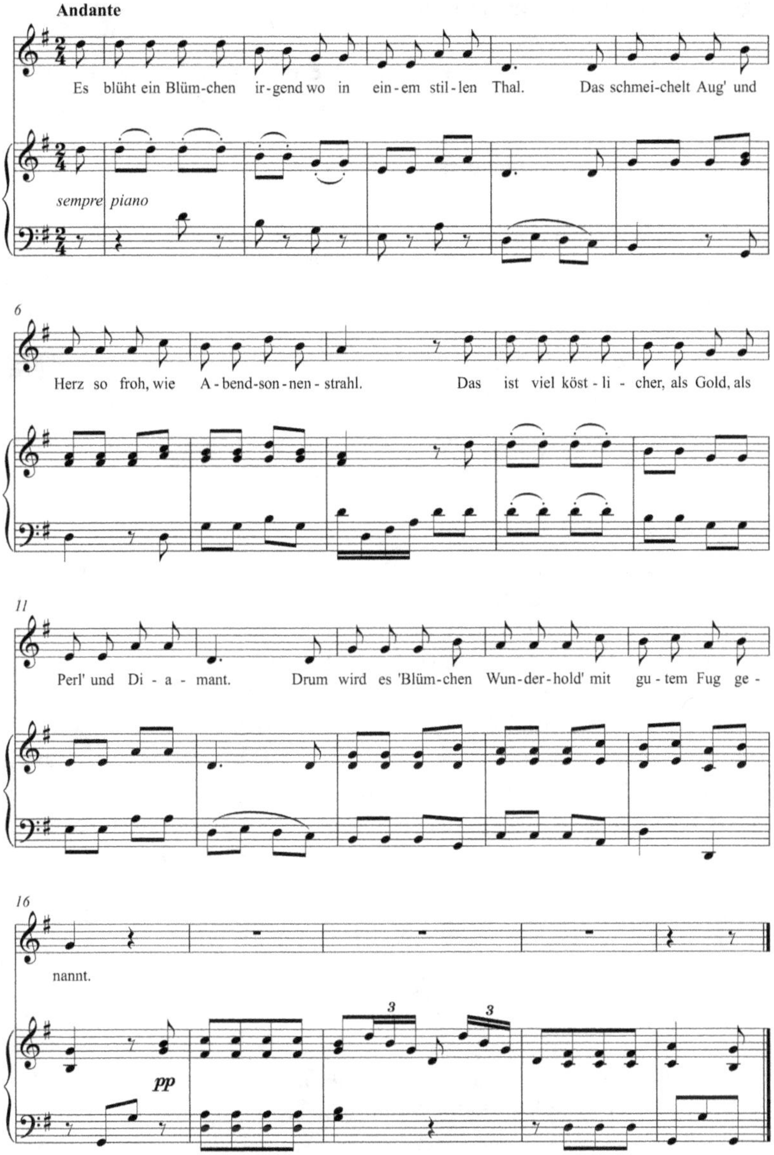

Example 2.1 Beethoven *Das Blümchen Wunderhold*

Both of these songs begin with the signal of a keyboard 'alberti bass' figuration, a texture which promises to support and lift the melodic line beyond a simple vocal capacity. The latter song is even retitled *Maigesang* in Beethoven's collection, as if to indicate the expanded nature of the setting. Thus across the various songs of his Op. 52 collection Beethoven seems to be creating an aesthetic balance between South and North, the sophisticated and the folk-like:

North German	*Viennese*
Op. 52 no. 1: *Urians Reise um die Welt* (Claudius)	Op. 52 no. 4: *Maigesang* (Goethe)
Op. 52 no. 7: *Marmotte* (Goethe)	Op. 52 no. 5: *Mollys Abschied* (Bürger)
Op. 52 no. 8: *Das Blümchen Wunderhold* (Bürger)	Op. 52 no. 6: *Die Liebe* (Lessing)

Left as three plus three in this way, the collection might suggest Beethoven wishing to honour both types of stylistic and aesthetic influence and to keep a clear distinction between them. However, if one includes the other two settings from Op. 52 it becomes more difficult to retain such boundaries. In both cases the first musical signals are not necessarily borne out by the rest of the song. In Beethoven's setting of *Das Liedchen von der Ruhe* (Op. 52 no. 3) the title's idea of a 'little song' and of 'rest' is conveyed by the matching hymn-like statements of the opening, with the lower part of the piano marking pauses for breath every two bars. The rise and fall of parallel thirds clearly suggests a communal rendering. Yet at the instant of the modulatory F# on the second quaver of bar 5 the piano accompaniment expands texturally and harmonically and the voice departs from its evenly patterned style into a more prosodic style of declamation (see Example 2.2).

The stylistic shifts in the setting of *Feuerfarb* (Op. 52 no. 2) are even more noticeable and confusing. The piano prelude establishes the definite steps and yodelling style of a *Tanzlied*; it is reminiscent of the skipping ritornelli that mark the end of each verse of *Marmotte* and *Das Blümchen Wunderhold*. Yet once the voice enters, the rhythmic patterning is used to power a different kind of melody, one which develops as a stream rather than as balancing arches, and indeed overflows into new music for the second verse of the poem. Once more it becomes difficult to decide between the basic distinction of strophic or through-composed. One has to try out a performance of the song over its eight verses to see whether the amount of repetition, as each pair of verses follows the same music, compensates for the flowing and diffuse nature of the voice's melodic line.

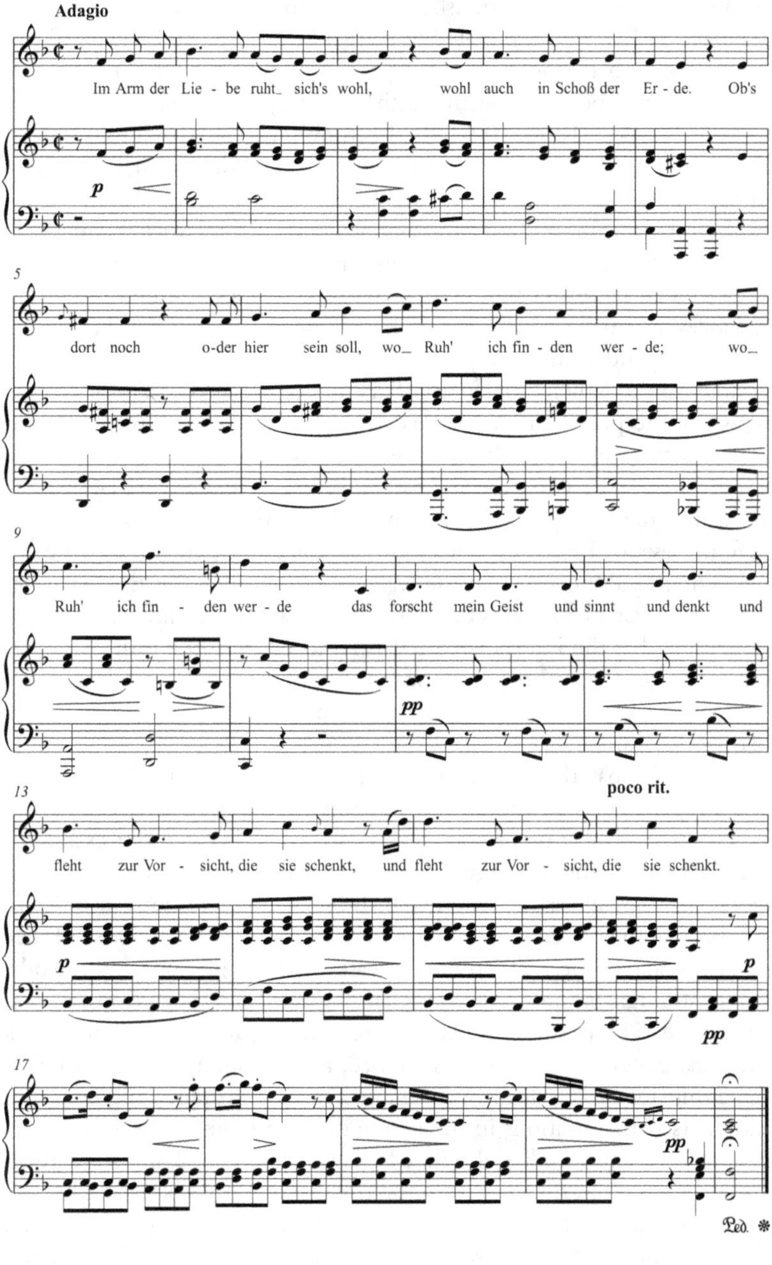

Example 2.2 Beethoven *Das Liedchen von der Ruhe*

The mixed nature of these songs reflects something of the slipperiness of their poems. When published in the Op. 52 collection, *Das Liedchen von der Ruhe* was attributed to Bürger rather than to Ueltzen (Reid, 2007, 91). In it the poet treats the peace of the lover's arms as a symbol for the greater peace of death; earth gives way to heaven 'as one drifts towards Paradise' (Reid, 2007, 91). Beethoven responds well to this troubling sense of the ineffable. 'Peace' seems given by the hymn-like solidity of the opening two-bar phrase, and by the matching two-bar sequence in the relative minor. But then the evenness of the two-bar phrases in Example 2.2 is disrupted by an interpolation of a vocal rest in bar 5, as though to reflect the internal twists of the poet's mind. The vocal cadences in bars 8 and 10 refer back to those in bars 2 and 4, but within a much expanded melodic parameter. From bar 11 two poetic lines are entirely run together, and bar 14 offers only a snatched breath before the repeat of the poetic line for a final vocal cadence at bar 16. Beethoven is thus setting up a parallel between the poetic theme and his musical grammar of 'rest'. The expected pauses for breath in bars 2 and 4 become set against the unexpected breath in bar 5 and then the struggle to keep definite rests or breathing points for the voice. One might see this as a dramatic impulse overtaking the lyricism of the song. Yet the *pianissimo* marking in bar 11 indicates that this is a drama of subtle implication. It is noticeable that the interpolated rest is removed from the fifth bar of the second verse, as Beethoven responds to the shifting stresses of the poem and allows prominence to the beloved's name, 'Elise', which is itself a play on Elysium.

It is clear that the poem can be taken as a light play on words, or as a deeper search to capture the mystery of experience; it can appear as sentimental ditty or profound metaphysics. What is more extraordinary is that Beethoven should explore and pass on that slipperiness so clearly in musical terms. One needs the strophic repetitions in order to sift through the patterns of phrasing to decide where the melodic essence of each shape resides. The postlude teases with simpler one-bar melodic shapes, though harmonically these are stretched into a four-and-a-half-bar phrase. The postlude invites one to listen again, rather than settling the aural pattern of what one has heard, as the melody's final resting on the dominant makes clear. In an important sense strophic song here rubs shoulders with variations in the nature of the listening experience. This is not just because of literal notated changes for verse 2 and subsequent verses. Apart from the change to the rhythm of the vocal line in bar 26, there are changes to the slurring in the keyboard part in bars 27 and 37 and in the postlude, as well as to the octave doubling in bar 26. But these hardly amount to developing variation in the accepted sense. The notion of variation comes in the invitation to listeners to question what the essence of the given material amounts to, as they track Beethoven's melody across the four stanzas of the poet's experience.

Feuerfarb, the remaining poem in Beethoven's Op. 52 collection, is even more confusing to the idle reader. One wonders whether its author, Sophie Mereau, the wife of the famous folk-inspired poet Clemens Brentano, had also been coming under Bürger's influence. Just as the natural phenomenon of a blossoming flower is made to symbolise a world of human virtue in *Das Blümchen Wunderhold*, so in *Feuerfarb* the phenomenon of colour becomes the occasion for a lengthy diatribe on what lasts and what fades. In *Wunderhold* the move between object and subject is aided by the clarity of the first image, 'a flower in a quiet valley'. But in *Feuerfarb* Mereau begins with a troubling abstraction, 'the colour of truth', her name for something which defies the experience of the senses. The title of the poem – 'Colour of flame' – gives the nearest indication of this colour's quality, though in referring to 'blazing sun' the poet makes clear that this colour is not to be experienced directly, unlike the colours of snow (innocence) or roses (love) which do not last. She suggests that anything the reader might be tempted to hold on to as a summary of experience will dissolve, or become a pointer to something else. There is a colour that lasts but we cannot see it. Given such a view of the poem, it becomes understandable why Beethoven should have teased the listener with a *Tanzlied* fragment as the prelude to his song. As the voice enters Beethoven weaves *Tanzlied* patterns – such as the skipping arpeggio of bar 4 or the cadential flourish of bar 8 – into bigger and bigger melodic arches. The postlude ends melodically with a simple *Tanzlied* turn, but it does not immediately stay in the memory as a summary of the previous melodic course. The ear has to pick out the turn from the next hearing of the two-verse musical strophe; once it enters the ear, the melodic shape can be heard everywhere (see Example 2.3).

Strophic repetition becomes a voyage of discovery approached in this way, for the listener as much as for the performer. The listener is encouraged to engage in a process of testing what has been heard and what might be heard next time round. Such a process is future related in encouraging speculation on what might emerge from further listening, but it also constantly circles back to the past, to a confirmation of the potential of what was first heard. In the *Feuerfarb* setting, this circling back is encapsulated in the very shape of the *Tanzlied* turn itself. Such melodic flourishes are often associated with a joy in the present; they spill out of North German *Im Volkston* songs, as with Hartmann's setting of Hölty's *Trinklied in Mai* or Reichardt's setting of Goethe's *Mit einem gemalten Band*. However, Beethoven here reworks such a familiar figure into an active symbol

Example 2.3 Beethoven *Feuerfarb*

of a different way of listening, forwards and backwards being bound together on one spot. In both micro and macro terms the song enacts a sense of time being constantly brought back to the present. Seen in this light, the strophic repetitions cease to be associated simply with fidelity to North German styles of song-setting; they become a vivid means of

Example 2.3 (Continued)

speculating how time works in music. Yet where the aesthetics of North German poets – and of Bürger in particular – remain entirely relevant is with the reliance on listeners to turn speculation into reality. It is only as such a song as *Feuerfarb* is responded to in real time that the comparison between future expectation and past memory gains substance. There is nothing solid that can be mapped out on the page, unlike with an actual theme and variations structure, only hints at a mixture of possibilities that require the construction or deconstruction of listening. As Bürger says, it requires a listener to respond to a 'brush stroke of magically rusty coloration'. If the response is forthcoming then the elusiveness of the material becomes in itself a source of celebration, since it opens the door between heard and imagined voices. What is not there takes on the significance of intended silences, silences which the listener is being invited to fill in.

Although *Das Blümchen Wunderhold* was admired at the time (Reid, 2007, 87), it is now hard to find any sympathetic commentary on Beethoven's Op. 52 collection. Few performers seem interested to sing these songs, perhaps because the Göttingen Hainbund sensibility seems so far from our own, and we have lost much of this intensity of listener engagement. Yet there is one song in the Op. 52 collection which can be said to retain its currency, Beethoven's setting of Goethe's *Mailied*. The poem gives the immediate impression of an infusion of energy; it builds on the raw power of alternating amphibrach and trochaic metres to underline the poet's assertion that joy, spring, love, song and dance belong in one ecstasy of youth:

Wie herrlich leuchtet
Mir die Natur!
Wie glänzt die Sonne!
Wie lacht die Flur!

Es dringen Blüten
Aus jedem Zweig
Und tausend Stimmen
Aus dem Gesträuch

Und Freud und Wonne
Aus jeder Brust.
O Erd', o Sonne!
O Glück, o Lust!

O Lieb, o Liebe!
So golden schön,
Wie Morgenwolken
Auf jenen Höhn!

Du segnest herrlich
Das frische Feld,

Im Blütendampfe
Die volle Welt.

O Mädchen, Mädchen,
Wie lieb ich dich!
Wie blickt dein Auge!
Wie liebst du mich!

So liebt die Lerche
Gesang und Luft,
Und Morgenblumen
Den Himmelsduft,

Wie ich dich liebe
Mit warmen Blut,
Die du mir Jugend
Und Freud und Mut

Zu neuen Liedern
Und Tänzen gibst.
Sei ewig glücklich,
Wie du mich liebst!
(Goethe, 1994, 10–12)

[How splendidly shines
Nature to me!
How the sun gleams
How the meadows laugh!

Buds spring forth
From every bough
And a thousand voices
Out of the bushes

And joy and rapture
From every heart.
O earth, O sun,
O bliss, O delight,

O love, O love,
So golden bright,

Like morning clouds
Up on the hills,

You bless with wonders
The fresh fields,
With flowery dew
The whole world!

O maiden, O maiden,
How I love you!
How your eyes sparkle!
How you love me!

As loves the lark
Song and sky,
And morning flowers
Love heavenly air,

So I love you
With warm blood,
As you give me youth
And joy and courage

For making new songs
And dances.
Be always happy,
As you love me.]
    (Author's translation)

Lines and stanzas overflow their boundaries; the three final strophes, for example, are tied into one sentence, but for the couplet on the end which directs the emotion straight at the beloved. 'All this joy will continue to overflow', the poet implies, 'as you love me' (Wie du mich liebst). Assertion mixes with appeal, for 'as you love me' brings hints of 'as long as you love me' or even 'provided you love me'. Since love is tied to the physical rhythms of spring and dance – and note the physicality of love suggested in the phrase 'mit warmen Blut' in the penultimate stanza – the passing of these might threaten the passing of love too, unless the song can somehow project a timelessness to offset the cumulative power of rhythm. Within the relentless gallop of the metre Goethe insinuates another kind of patterning, one of rhyme. Although the poem follows a basic rhyming scheme of *abcb* throughout, with the emphasis again upon directing forwards to the repeated *b*, there are gradations of rhyme within the pattern of verses that create key moments where all suddenly seems to fall into place. In the third verse the rhyme intensifies to *abab*, so underlining the exclamation 'O Glück, o Lust!' In the sixth verse, the Papageno-Papagena-like pairing of 'dich' and 'mich' (thee and me), is rammed home by the repetition of 'Wie' at the start of three out of the four lines. By inserting these moments of exaggerated rhyme into the third and sixth verses, Goethe creates a bird's eye view from which to mark the passing of time before the concluding couplet of the ninth verse. The poet's experience is subject to a subtle ordering that hints at the operation of memory on his part. This is not actually a song to be sung in the hedgerows – as the Göttinger Hainbund aspired to create – but a song for salon appreciation, where speculation on how perceptions of time may shift and change can be savoured as a matter of play.

For Schiller, this urge to abstract play (*Spieltrieb*) was vital to the integrity of art and its claim to timelessness (Schiller, 1967, 97). He would undoubtedly place Goethe's *Mailied* on an entirely different artistic level from the other poems in the Op. 52 collection, including Goethe's own buffooning *Marmotte*. Yet for Beethoven there are distinct aspects of continuity between his setting of this poem and the rest of Op. 52. In certain ways Beethoven responds directly to Goethe's way of controlling the flow of this poem. He elides the individual strophe to create a three-verse superstructure; the song is presented as three meta-strophes which, as in Goethe's poem, aim towards landmarks of completion in verses 3, 6 and 9. This end-directed energy is emphasised by the *ABB* pattern of repetition within each meta-strophe, and by the extra musical and textual repetitions inserted into the ninth and final verse. But there is also much in the song that relates to the naïve *Tanzlied* aspects of *Feuerfarb*. The keyboard begins with obsessive circles, both in the circling melodic figures and the overall shape of the 14-bar prelude, which turns back upon itself like a snake eating its own tail. The forward drive of the song is thus confronted with a simultaneous backwards impulse. And despite the ensuing *ABB* pattern of the meta-strophe the emphasis continues to fall back upon *A*. The subdominant harmony that marks the opening of the prelude and the voice's entry recurs prominently in the *B* sections of the meta-strophe, at bars 24 and 32, as well as in the interludes. In bars 43 and 47 the lean to the subdominant is interpolated in extra four-bar phrases, after the dominant-tonic alternations of bars 38–41. The sense of relaxation associated with the subdominant pervades the song with cumulative effect. Apart from the impact of the song's strophic repetitions, the newly inserted phrases of the final verse re-emphasise the subdominant in bars 113 and 117 to highlight the crucial word 'ewig'. The C and A♭

which encircle the tonic triad within the melodic turn of the opening thus retain their presence across the song through being reconfigured as a harmonic signpost. The linear is shown to be projected vertically, melody becomes harmony, time becomes space. In this sense the subdominant leans on the repetitions of 'ewig' (eternally), in bars 113 and 117, acquire a particular agency. Goethe's 'Sei *ewig* glücklich' is given the resonance of a plagal 'Amen', before the postlude skips away with perfect cadences. Though this spatial perspective is consummated at the end of the song, in a sense it is present in the simultaneity of the very first melodic-harmonic 'touch' of the prelude, so that the formal process can be seen as to fold back upon itself in another version of the snake eating its own tail. In stylistic terms this setting represents a sophisticated Viennese keyboard song, yet in essence it follows the circular pattern of Beethoven's *Das Blümchen Wunderhold*. Bürger's aesthetic of the magic of the moment, as summed up musically in a melodic dancing on the spot, can be heard to infect all of the Op. 52 songs – if the listener chooses to treasure such 'ditty-ness'.

Beethoven's *Maigesang* confirms that 'ditty-ness' can be treasured as much in a developed keyboard song as in a North German-style *Im Volkston* evocation. One might say it can be treasured more, since the choice to home in on the simplest melodic configuration – a dancing on the spot – is made in the context of alternative musical perspectives. *Maigesang* remains a through-composed conception, even if the composer uses this to invoke aspects of circularity. The change in the pattern of repetitions for the song's ninth verse signals a formal open-endedness which distances the song from its poetic origins as a strophic Lied. It is significant perhaps that Beethoven also adapted this music to fit the words of an aria, 'O welch ein Leben', for the *Singspiel Die schöne Schusterin* (Reid, 2007, 206; Friedlaender, 1896, 180). One can imagine the final triumphant vocal repetitions and the flourishes of the postlude drawing enthusiastic applause from a theatre audience.

Beethoven's setting of Bürger's *Gegenliebe* shows even more obvious signs of operatic influence. Apart from pairing this song with the aria-like *Seufzer eines Ungeliebten*, Beethoven creates a decidedly theatrical moment in the passage before the return of the song's first section in bar 132. With the lingering repetitions of 'Wüßt' ich', he makes the singer seem to wait upon an audience response before the restart of the main melody. The voice's faltering stop on the seventh over the dominant in bar 130 is reminiscent of Mozart's comical setting of Papageno's 'Nun, ich warte noch' in *Die Zauberflöte*, when Papageno seeks the audience's aid in conjuring up his Papagena. Although he does not actually bring his song to a halt, Beethoven creates an urgency about the performance of strophic repetition that transcends the immediate context. Overall the setting of

Gegenliebe traces a regular four-fold periodic structure that reflects the four-strophe shape of Bürger's poem. Whilst the first section, and the third which repeats it, follow a closely patterned 24-bar structure of *ABA1* phrasing, even the more developmental second and fourth sections conform to the song's larger sense of periodicity; the second section (beginning from the second half of bar 110) outlines a 22-bar paragraph on the dominant, while the fourth section (beginning from the second half of bar 156) expands codetta-like into a 26-bar period ending on the tonic. Unlike in a sonata-form style structure, the lengths of sections seem pre-determined; they are measured out as strophes, even if internally the material is subject to strong developmental tendencies. The question then becomes how the song will be heard, whether as a true 'ditty' in the Bürger-derived sense, or as a sophisticated reflection of character such as might be heard on the stage.

For evoking the sound of 'popular songs' under the linden tree, Bürger makes it clear that there needs to be an implied chain reaction between what is inherent in the ditties themselves and the sensibility that the poet brings, a chain reaction which he then appeals for others to join in with. Once the simple step-wise rise and fall at the beginning of Beethoven's *Gegenliebe* gives way to circling variation from the ninth bar, the raw 'ditty-ness' of his setting might begin to fade from view, except that the composer inserts a pause and a sliding vocal inflection into the song's sixteenth bar (bar 102) to make an exaggerated 'all-together-now' appeal to the listener for the repeat of the first eight-bar phrase. As *A* alternates with *B*, the developmental impulses of the latter are shown to be countermanded by an emphatic stop and return to the former. It is as though Beethoven intervenes in his own song and invites the listener to join him in singing back his first melody. Just as the song's largest four-section shape is presented as closing back upon the repeat of the first section in bar 132, the *ABA* of the first section closes back upon *A* as though the whole song is to be heard as residing in one such exaggeratedly simple profile.

Given the extreme degree of repetition, development and variation to which Beethoven subjects the eight-bar opening of *Gegenliebe*, both in this song-setting and in the *Choral Fantasy*, it is easy to pass over what this eight-bar shape might represent in itself. It is tempting to view it like some annoying riff that plays obsessively in the brain without pausing to consider whether it could actually represent a tuneful melody in and of itself. In terms of Bürger's *Gegenliebe*, the eight bars correspond to one verse of his poem, even though both verses one and two of the poem run on to the next and only verse three is end-punctuated. Bürger makes the strophes succeed each other swiftly in the hope that 'love nourishes a loving response' (Reid, 2007, 255). What the poet enacts is the hoped-for alternation between a lover and his beloved, love responding to love, strophe to strophe, melody to melody. From this melodic contagion the poet conceives a 'dying ember' being fanned into a 'raging fire'. But first is the request for the beloved to return just the 'tiniest part' of what he feels (see verse 1); the details of the melody are to be heard and 'given back' (verse 2). Beethoven's melody is full of cues for repetition in its generative shaping. Yet it is interesting how Beethoven indicates a melodic step away for the poem's second verse (see the *B* insertion) before a repeat is allowed for the third verse. It seems a certain effort of memory and will is needed if the infectious nature of the opening tune is to be fully realised. As discussed in Chapter 4, the composer plays with a different version of this *A-B* alternation in the *Choral Fantasy*, where the repeat of *A* follows after just four bars of *B*; the beloved seems nearer at hand, as befits the celebratory optimism of the *Choral Fantasy's* poetic text. If the Ninth Symphony's 'Ode to Joy' melody is allowed to be part of this melodic chain reaction, then its *ABB* structure suggests how the beloved is one step further away from immediately joining in with the eight-bar strophe, thus requiring greater efforts still of will and imagination.

In playing with different performances of melody in this way, Beethoven creates his own conversation with Bürger's aspirations for communion in song. The particular nature of this melodic type becomes significant as a possible way of understanding Beethoven's ideals for songwriting as a whole. Looking at the profile of *Gegenliebe's* characteristic opening, one notes it is made up of three melodic turns which circle around E, B and D in turn. On repeat, the circles around E and B are followed by a closing 'hop' to C. Although, departing from the ubiquitous step-wise movement, this last figure pulls the phrase into a larger E-D-B-C turn, so completing the 'snake eating its own tail' image that was so prominent in *Maigesang*. The poise of 'one note above, one note below' evokes a melody complete in itself whilst open to apparently endless revolutions. And here the evocation of a melodic circle has the potential to work as a literal eight-bar tune (see Example 2.4).

Although Beethoven does not often create such compact strophes, apart from the songs of *An die ferne Geliebte*, the effort to model extreme melodic concision seems to have been a recurring aspect of his songwriting. Beethoven often ends even extremely diffuse songs with some kind of melodic tag, as though to indicate a reversion to the ideal of song as a magnified 'brush stroke'. The second setting of Tiedge's *An die Hoffnung* gives such an example (see Example 2.5).

Example 2.4 Beethoven *Gegenliebe*, bars 1–8

Example 2.5 Beethoven *An die Hoffnung* (second version), final two bars

Despite coming right at the end of the song, the melodic sigh hovers as though indicating the possibility of starting again. In this case, the summary is an add-on, both textually and musically, to the body of the song; the tag is detachable. But in others the tag becomes the song, or the song the tag, so fulfilling the desire to find meaning in the merest 'brush stroke'. Beethoven's setting of Goethe's 'Ich denke dein' begins with what might be a quotation from the closing figure of the eight-bar strophe in *Gegenliebe* (Example 2.4). This cadential figure is echoed in almost every bar of the vocal melody (in bars 4, 5, 7, 8, 10, 11), as well as in the melodic summaries of the postlude, so that the song can be heard as a literal expansion and contraction upon one 'dying fall':

Example 2.6 Beethoven 'Ich denke dein'

Beethoven made this strophe the subject of a series of variations for piano duet. The most revealing melodic exploration comes with the third variation, which divides the original melody between the pianists. The *secondo* performer begins with repetitions of the cadential tag whilst the *primo* player is tasked with turning tag into melody:

Example 2.7 Beethoven 'Ich denke dein', third variation, bars 1–6

It is as though Beethoven wishes to show the cliché of song-ending being carried into fully fledged melodic flight, in a collaborative act of hearing and responding.

There are particular reasons why such a mode of melodic configuration was appropriate to Goethe's 'Ich denke dein' poem. Goethe's lyric is an elaboration upon his response to Zelter's song-setting of a Friederike Brun poem, which is in its turn a response to a poem of Matthisson. All three poems – of Goethe, Brun and Matthisson – begin with the same 'Ich denke dein' tag. Goethe kept to the same poetic rhythmic structure as Brun, as inspired by Zelter's musical rendering, but Brun expanded greatly on the compact patterns of Matthisson's original. Matthisson uses the immediate iambic rhythm and the rhyming sound of the 'Ich denke dein' phrase to govern his poem as a whole, except for the skipping amphibrach inserted into the third and fourth lines of each strophe. Each of Matthisson's four strophes follows this same pattern, including beginning with the 'Ich denke dein' phrase, so that by the end of the poem there have been 12 occurrences of the same 'ein' sound. The final verse varies the opening phrase to 'O denke mein', so that 'mein' can be rhymed with 'dein' as the final word of the poem:

Ich denke dein
Wenn durch den Hain
Der Nachtigallen
Akkorde schallen.
Wann denkst du mein?

Ich denke dein
Im Dämmerschein
Der Abendhelle
Am Schattenquelle.
Wo denkst du mein?

Ich denke dein
Mit süsser Pein,
Mit bangem Sehnen
Und heissen Tränen.
Wie denkst du mein?

O denke mein
Bis zum Verein
Auf besserm Sterne!
In jeder Ferne
Denk' ich nur dein!
        (Matthisson, 1815,
            209–210)

[I think of you
When through the grove
The nightingale
Pours out chords.
When do you think of me?

I think of you
In the twilight
Of an evening glow
By the shadowed spring.
Where do you think of me?

I think of you
With sweet torment,
With fearful sighs
And hot tears.
How do you think of me?

O think of me
Until we are together
On a better star!
Far away
I think only of you.]
     (Author's translation)

The poet's obsessive use of rhyme asserts the communion of lover and beloved, however great the distance between them ('Ferne'). The intensity of the poetic structure turns what might seem a lovers' platitude into a definite statement of aesthetic intent: in the lyric, poet and listener become one. Brun's 'Ich denke dein' elaborates hugely on the contrasting scenes of life in which the poet dreams of the beloved; she uses more varied rhymes and expanded line lengths to indicate her enthusiastic response to Matthisson. Her poetry spills over with a rhythmic ebb and flow that matches the wave imagery of her second verse:

Ich denke dein, wenn sich der Weltmeer tönend
Gen Himmel hebt,
Und vor der Wogen Wut das Ufer stöhnend
Zurückebebt.
                    (Brun, 1795, 44)

[I think of you, when the roaring ocean lifts itself
Towards heaven
And as the groaning shore before the rage of the waves
Staggers back.]
                    (Author's translation).

Goethe responds in his turn by keeping Brun's rhythms, but varying the poem's 'head motif' as though probing the connection between internal and external realities; 'I think of you' transmutes into 'I see you', 'I hear you', before the final assertion 'I am with you'. There is a greater sense of structure in Goethe's approach, as if he takes the poetic chain reaction as an opportunity to critique the original (Sternfeld, 1954, 107). It is interesting that in responding to Goethe's poem Beethoven chooses to replace the poem's strophic repetitions with an exploratory theme and variations structure. Yet in melodic essentials, Beethoven continues to hark back to the obsessive rhyming of Matthisson's original poem. Such melodic concision becomes even more striking if one turns to Beethoven's setting of Matthisson's 'Ich denke dein', which followed in 1809, four years after the piano duet variations. Beethoven's Matthisson setting once more begins with an ending, with the melodic summary of a compact cadential figure. Without the repeating echoes, from the piano in bars 13 and 14, from the voice in bars 16 to 18, the musical strophe would consist of only eight bars. Yet given the emphatic focus upon the two-bar figure for the three words 'Ich denke dein' themselves, an eight-bar shape comes to seem quite expansive. The whole song seems designed to turn upon a pin head, spinning back to its opening before thoughts can stray too far from the poet's initial assertion:

Example 2.8 Beethoven *Andenken*, bars 7–18

'I think of you when . . .' – in Beethoven's setting the following details are shown to be almost irrelevant given the poet's claim of instant communion with the beloved. The assertion of communion remains paramount, almost to the point that the song is swallowed up in the hammering upon a single figure. Strophic repetitions are here relativised as an outworking of a more basic musical and poetic principle: if an instant can be captured and held in the memory, then it can be told countless times. The achievement of melodic concision, the clear imprint on memory, will allow the song to reach into any distances, whether these are conceived as distances of time or place. The beloved, the one who is supposed to respond to the poet's utterance, is placed at a distance in the 'Ich denke dein' poetry precisely so that she can test whether the poet has succeeded in capturing a moment across space and time. The immediate and the distant are jumbled together in all of the 'Ich denke dein' poems, though Matthisson sums it up most ambitiously of all in the final verse of his poem as he projects his union with the beloved to a 'better star'. Beethoven responds by releasing a string of developmental sequences for the final verse of his setting; melodic concision is replaced by a melodic stream, strophic repetitions by through-composed flight. Each time the melodic course seems to subside towards a point of cadence, it is swept forwards by new points of variation. It is only when a close is seemingly imposed by the carefully spaced perfect cadences of the postlude that memory is given the opportunity to test itself. From the silences following the piano's cadences the voice reintroduces its own summary of closure, in a manner that re-invokes the song's first pinhead focus on D:

Example 2.9 Beethoven *Andenken*, bars 76–82

One might think of Beethoven's 'Ich denke dein' setting chiming with T. S. Eliot's words in 'Little Gidding' from *Four Quartets* (Eliot, 1968): 'Every phrase and every sentence is an end and a beginning, / Every poem an epitaph'. 'East Coker', the second 'quartet', is given two bookend statements, 'In my beginning is my end' and 'In my end is my beginning', which seek to pull the poem to a single point. Throughout *Four Quartets*, Eliot teases the listener by overlaying statements that appeal to an eternal present, while requiring an effort of memory on the listener's part to sift the repeated statements for the kernels of sound and meaning that will allow the experience of present-ness to be confirmed.

> To be conscious is not to be in time
> But only in time can the moment in the rose-garden.
> The moment in the arbour where the rain beat,
> The moment in the draughty church at smokefall
> Be remembered; involved with past and future.
> Only through time time is conquered.
>
> ('Burnt Norton')

The self-consciousness of the subject-matter, in which the lyricist's wish to transcend time is constantly impressed upon the listener, is part of the appeal to make the listener's imagination take the impossible step of working in time to make time stand still. Similarly poets' use of the 'I think of you' tag is a signal that the listener must be active in configuring what a bringing together across time and space might mean. The repetition of the same tag in a spiral of varying poetic contexts is designed both to open up awareness of difference and distance in an apparently centrifugal motion, and to bring those contexts back, centripetally, to one point – 'the still point of the turning world' ('Burnt Norton'). To use another analogy, the strophes of the 'Ich denke dein' lyrics work like a concertina, taking in air to expand the view as far as possible before compressing back to one point of refrain. The patterns of repetition are thus energised and become part of the subject-matter of the poem; they become a crucial testing-ground for the poet's assertion that the listener-beloved is near.

In both of his 'Ich denke dein' settings Beethoven can be seen to respond to this poetic challenge to heighten the meaning of strophic repetition, in his first setting through combining it with techniques of variation, in his second with techniques of development. For Beethoven's setting of Matthisson's 'Ich denke dein' is technically speaking a 'Gesang', the song being powered by a keyboard-based alternation of tonic and dominant harmonies over a tonic pedal. The listener is drawn to wait for the outcome of a sonata-like play between small-scale harmonic alternation, and the larger tonal pull of the imperfect cadences in bars 6, 12 and 18. The resolution of these imperfect cadences (recurring in bars 25, 29, 38 and 44) does not happen within the compass of each 12-bar strophe, but is delayed to the perfect cadence which marks the beginning of the next strophe (in bars 20 and 33), and in the end to the expanded coda-style dominant-tonic alternations of the final fourth verse. The attention of the listener is constantly projected forwards, but (as already discussed) only so that it can be brought back to the melodic pinpoint from which it began. Thus the listener's attention is thrown between future and past, between detail and whole. If the song is to be heard strophically it has to be done so in retrospect, as the listener reimagines the perfect cadence at the beginning of each new strophe as an ending as well as a beginning, inspired by how the song turns back upon itself in the closing measures. The listener is thus invited to treasure and remember the song as a 'Lied', even while it behaves as a 'Gesang'.

Beethoven composed a whole group of songs in 1809 that share the poetic notion of an appeal for response from a distant beloved. Apart from his setting of Matthisson's 'Ich denke dein' from that same time, the composer turned to poems from the *Blümchen der Einsamkeit* (Flowers of Loneliness) collection of Christian Ludwig Reissig. Their titles – *Lied aus der Ferne, Der Jüngling in der Fremde, An den fernen Geliebten* – make them seem like poetic foreshadows of Beethoven's song-cycle *An die ferne Geliebte*. The resonance of such subject matter for the composer's personal life is clear (Tyson, 1973, 129; Cooper, 1990, 49–51), but this should not downplay the aesthetic attraction that Beethoven seems to have felt for the opportunity to highlight musical ideas of presence and absence. Although Beethoven said that a song-composer should rise above the poet (Hamburger, 1951, 223), in this instance he seems to have been content to pour energy into animating a familiar poetic vocabulary, even a string of clichéd images of how to conjure an absent beloved. The final two verses of Reissig's *An den fernen Geliebten* are reminiscent of the 'Ich denke dein' poems in their reference to the magical effect of evening light:

Wenn sanft eine Lüftchen deine Locken kräuselt
Im Mondenlicht,
Das ist mein Geist, der flehend dich umsäuselt:
Vergiss mein nicht.

Wirst du im Vollmondschein dich nach mir sehnen,
Wie Zephyrs Weh'n
Wird dir's melodisch durch die Lüfte tönen:
'Auf Wiedersehn'.

(Reissig, 1809, 44)

[When softly a breeze rumples your curls
By moonlight,
That is my spirit, beseechingly murmuring
Do not forget me.

If in full moonlight you were ever to yearn for me,
Like a zephyr's sigh
Would sound melodiously through the air to you:
'Until we meet again'.]

(Author's translation)

These verses also chime in with the final poem of Jeitteles's *An die ferne Geliebte* cycle, the specific scene where the poet imagines the beloved receiving his message of love:

Wenn das Dämmerungsrot dann ziehet
Nach dem stillen blauen See,
Und sein letzter Strahl verglühet
Hinter jener Bergeshöh';

Und du singst, was ich gesungen,
Was mir aus der vollen Brust
Ohne Kunstgepräng' erklungen,
Nur der Sehnsucht sich bewusst.

[When the twilight red then draws
Towards the still blue lake,
And its last ray sinks
Behind those mountain peaks;

And you sing, what I sang,
What sounded out of my full breast
Without the splendour of art,
Conscious only of longing.]

(Author's translation)

From both poems comes the notion that with twilight comes a new acuity to sound, so that song can be conjured from a breath or a sigh. Such a sigh passes across mountains in Jeitteles's imagination or drifts on the breeze in Reissig's, for the beloved to reconceive melodically ('melodisch'). The Jeitteles cycle offers a whole sequence of imagery

for this process of conjuration. But even with Reissig's simpler material, Beethoven seizes the opportunity to probe what is implied by the
poet's notion of 'melodisch'. With the subject matter of *An den fernen
Geliebten* one might expect the composer to provide a heart-warming
arching melody such as he composes for Reissig's *Lied aus der Ferne*. In
his setting of *Lied aus der Ferne* melismatic sigh-shapes pervade almost
every bar, sometimes lifting sometimes falling, to create a clear momentum of flight. Beethoven went on to compose a second much expanded
setting of this poem, now re-titled *Gesang aus der Ferne*, where the sense
of melodic impulsion coming from rising sigh-shapes creates the most
extraordinary, quasi-operatic momentum. Yet Beethoven also seems to
have valued his original winsome melody; he recast it as a setting of a
different Reissig poem, *Der Jüngling in der Fremde*. Beethoven does not
always choose to enhance his appeal to the beloved through melodic
expansion. With *An den fernen Geliebten* Beethoven strips the vocal line
back to the barest ingredients. The rippling keyboard texture indicates a
sense of momentum, but the vocal line sticks obsessively to the opening
D-B melodic third (see Example 2.10).

In this example the composer passes on the sound of sighs, melodi-
cised into a falling third, but without offering full melodic flight. The
insistent repetition, starting and ending on D-B within the four-bar
phrase, curtails a sense of melodic rise and fall, or even of circling.
The raw interval, the building brick of melody, juts out from the
vocal line. In the extension that Beethoven added to the close in his
revised version of the setting, the third emerges more clearly as the
summary for the whole, though in this instance the third is not a
generative figure, like the compact cadential motif at the head of 'Ich
denke dein'. Instead the third comes across as an irreducible element
(see Example 2.11). One might say that in tribute to the poetic content of *An den fernen Geliebten* Beethoven refuses to move beyond sighs
in his setting, even if in their inner details each sigh becomes a different kind of story. The single D-B interval hovers between vertical
and horizontal presentations in a way that creates movement within
the sounding object. In Example 2.10 the horizontal is shown to be
drawn from the vertical at the opening of the song, whereas towards
the end of the first four-bar phrase the melodic D (at the end of
bar 3) is separated out horizontally from B and aligned harmonically
with the dominant rather than the tonic G. In Example 2.11 the final
flourish from the piano brings the B-G interval into the closest hori-
zontal-vertical nexus yet, as confirmation of the intervallic play with
space-time configurations.

Example 2.10 Beethoven *An den fernen Geliebten*

Example 2.11 Beethoven *An den fernen Geliebten* (second version), final three bars

Strophic repetition is a key part of this song's conception from its opening anacrusis; for it is only as the placement of each detail of the piano texture is checked against the vocal line that the song's intervallic play is exposed. Each time the strophe comes round such details are heard afresh and become part of the process of melodic conjuration. Beethoven finds space within the simplest strophic song for his own particular play with detail and whole, time and space.

It is tempting to use the overlap of title between Reissig's *An den fernen Geliebten* and Jeitteles's *An die ferne Geliebte* as a reason for presenting Beethoven's Reissig setting as a testing ground for his highly sophisticated treatment of strophic repetition in his song-cycle. If Beethoven commissioned Jeitteles's poems, as some have believed (Cooper, 1990, 50), then the coincidence of title may indeed have been intentional. Even so, the chronological gap might seem too far. Whilst 1809 is still seen as the height of Beethoven's middle period, the composition of *An die ferne Geliebte* in 1815 brings one to the brink of the late style and even heralds it, to use Kerman's term (Tyson, 1973, 129). Yet there are aspects of melodic atomisation in Beethoven's setting of the Reissig poem that connect to the innovations of the late style. Michael Spitzer speaks of the 'enormous amount of information' that Beethoven packs into single points in his late style (Spitzer, 2006, 229). One of the examples he picks out concerns caesuras, which can be defined as 'pauses in a line of verse, usually near the middle' (*Chambers English Dictionary*). In his late style Beethoven activates such an aspect of musical grammar to give a 'cognitive jolt of awareness', so that the caesura interrupts even while it institutes metrical patterns. It becomes like a 'black hole' or 'exit hole' through which the listener can pass in and out of the music (Spitzer, 2006, 229). In making the voice come to a pause in bar 4 with the D-B interval of the opening, in his setting *An den fernen Geliebten*, Beethoven prepares just such a 'jolt' for the listener. An impression of leaning forwards at the point of cadence coincides with an impression of travelling backwards, to bring the mind of the listener, potentially, to a juddering halt. Just as Spitzer talks of Beethoven in the late style creating an 'allegorical objectification of convention . . . so that we "see" it' (Spitzer, 2006, 229), here the intervallic third becomes almost an object of sight, in the sense of being held up to be viewed from different sides.

Just before embarking on his late song-cycle Beethoven returned to Reissig's *Blümchen der Einsamkeiten* collection to set *Sehnsucht*, a song that offers a further link between the earlier and later 'distant beloved' songs. *Sehnsucht* is a far more sophisticated melodic evocation than *An den fernen Geliebten*, but there is still the explicit play with the melodic interval of a falling third, in this case the opening G#-E. The piano prelude offers

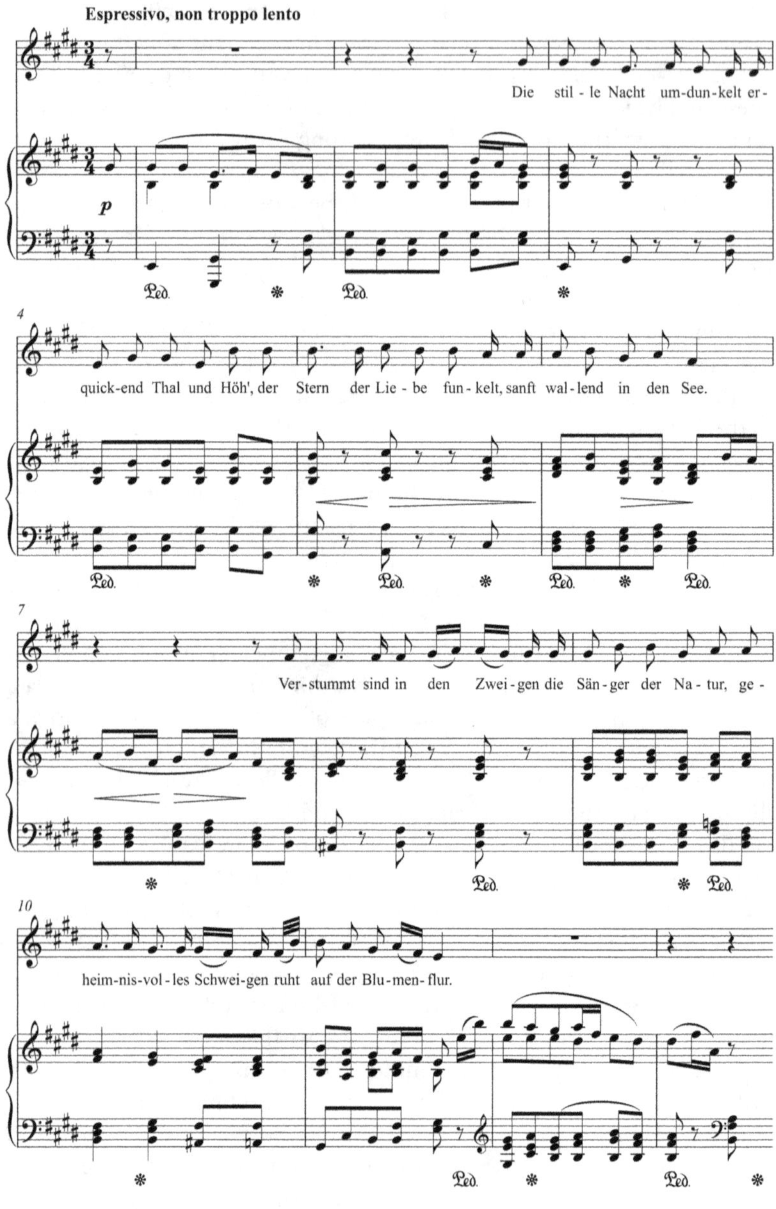

Example 2.12 Beethoven *Sehnsucht*, bars 1–13

multiple melodic and harmonic reflections of these pitches, so that the voice enters across a confusion of horizontal and vertical dimensions. The elision of the downbeat to bar 2 conveys an immediate sense of temporal suspension, a blurring that is echoed at every subsequent downbeat until the end of the strophe in bar 11. It is only at this final point that the song's melodic and harmonic profiles are shown to resolve into a clear cadential formula. This articulation of closure is immediately undermined by the piano interlude in bars 12 and 13. Whilst the piano echoes the melodic close upon the tonic on the third beat of bar 12, the movement to closure is blurred by the repeated dominant of the lowest part, followed by a further harmonic elision into bar 13 (see Example 2.12).

The vocal line emerges from an instrumental tintinnabulation of sound at the beginning of the song's second verse. Across the song Beethoven offers a three-fold strophic repetition, but the continuing harmonic blurring of the downbeat ensures that the song's larger melodic profile remains in flux, as confirmed by variations within the piano texture. In his longing the poet asks to be deceived by a 'blissful dream' (Reid, 2007, 247); an image has to take the place of presence as the beloved flees from him. This might seem a platitude of hopeless longing, but Beethoven turns it into a specific test of the imagination. As though in response to the piano's variations, Beethoven instructs the singer to pick out and emphasise particular points in the vocal line through the insertion of rests. In the second verse this involves highlighting the resolution to the cadence in bar 22. But in the third verse two shapes are picked out (bars 27 and 30) which show the vocal line revolving in apparently aimless sequences of thirds:

Example 2.13 Beethoven *Sehnsucht*, bar 27 (vocal line)

Example 2.14 Beethoven *Sehnsucht*, bar 30 (vocal line)

These examples sum up the forwards and backwards oscillation which creates a kind of hiatus in the song's melodic progress. A stasis is suggested at the heart of the song, a denial of movement that undermines the notion of longing's fulfilment. At the close of the song even the stable identity of the G#-E intervallic third seems to drift away as the G# is removed from the piano's final echo of the vocal cadence. Except that the G# is slipped in again at the last moment as part of a vertical rather than melodic entity, to reconfirm the simultaneity of impulse that was impressed upon by the listener by the opening of the song:

Example 2.15 Beethoven *Sehnsucht*, bars 33–34

In Reissig's poem the appearance of the beloved is summoned out of stillness, silence and darkness. Beethoven goes a step further and seems to use a musical sequence to deny narrative. As the song expands with processes of strophic variation, the unit of attention seems to get smaller and smaller until only the vertical G#-E interval is left. The travelling inwards of the poem – with its details of tears, sleep and dream – becomes the occasion for Beethoven to experiment with new ways of listening, listening that in its intensity can offer its own way of drawing the listener near.

The 'concertina' techniques perfected in this setting of Reissig's *Sehnsucht* – the simultaneous expansion and contraction of musical dimensions – become, arguably, the bedrock of Beethoven's *An die ferne Geliebte* song-cycle. Whilst *Sehnsucht* can be heard to revolve around the harmonic and melodic permutations of the G#-E intervallic third, *An die ferne Geliebte* picks up an initial G-Eb building block to define a tonal as well as a harmonic-melodic *modus operandi*. The scope of the interval is set out in the cycle's opening three bars, where the Eb-G focus of the piano in bar 2 arises as a movement from the statement of the Eb tonic triad in bar 1, to be then projected forwards as the substance of the voice's melodic sigh of bar 3. The single interval, Eb-G, is extracted from its melodic and harmonic surroundings only to be absorbed into the sounding of the submediant, C minor, on the second beat of bar 3. Spaces open up around the interval, even as insistence on the same pitches might imply a kind of diminution:

Example 2.16 Beethoven *An die ferne Geliebte*, bars 1–9

Bar 3 marks the beginning of a chain reaction, where the initial G-E♭ is extended via the addition of further thirds – C, A♭, F – each working in simultaneous melodic and harmonic dimensions. From the furthest point of F, as heard harmonically in bar 4 and melodically in bar 5, the strophe works its way back to melodic and harmonic closure on G-E♭. The melodic-harmonic formulations of bar 7 and bar 9 bring near echoes of the piano's G-E♭ statements of bar 2. The chain has opened, it now closes back. The four-fold revolution of the strophe that swiftly succeeds this first eight-bar phrase works like a magnification of this detailed chain reaction; each strophe could be heard as spiralling backwards as much as spiralling forwards.

Jeitteles speaks of how the poet's sighs and looks speed ardently towards the beloved, but then rebound on meeting the barrier of mountains. Beethoven sets the poet's appeal for song to transcend time and space in a musical context where time and space are gauged via the building block of the intervallic third. This building block becomes more prominent as the cycle progresses rather than less. The moment as the door opens to the second song, the moment when the poet seeks to transport himself in his imagination across the mountains to the peaceful valley the other side, is highlighted by Beethoven as an opportunity to draw the intervallic third out of the melodic sequence. The G-E♭ in bar 52 connects aurally with the vertical sonority of bar 2 but surrounded by silences rather than any other motivic markers. Unlike the silences that usually follow a song's final cadence, which can be extended at will to allow echoes of the voice's closing melodic phrase, the pauses within this piano transition are articulated to last only for a snatch of time. The exchange of the G-E♭ third for the G-B in bar 54 is presented as a pure manipulation of third-ness. The ear is invited to contract from the third to the single note, and then to reconstruct the third in a different tonal parameter. The focus on G continues throughout the second song, most clearly with the voice's monotonous intoning of G for the length of the second verse. The shape of the second song's piano prelude, where the G-B focus tips back to G, continues to determine much of the song:

Example 2.17 Beethoven *An die ferne Geliebte*, bars 51–59

The subsequent step downwards to link G with E, from bars 71 to 72, both acts to introduce the move to the subdominant C major for the second verse, and to refer back to the moment of transition from the first song. The spatial resonance of reversing the direction of the intervallic third, from above the pivot G to back below, is made fully prominent in bars 100–101 in the transition to the cycle's third song. The moment when the drop to E♭ is reintroduced melodically in bar 101 offers to connect with the C minor sonority on the second beat of bar 3 of the cycle (see Example 2.16).

With this aural connection, the A♭ tonality of the third song can be heard as a large-scale projection of the melodic-harmonic extension beyond G-E♭ to C-A♭ in bars 3 and 4 of the cycle's first song. The cycle's melodic-harmonic-tonal steps can all seem to be interrelated, provided the ear can project the intervallic third across such wide dimensions. The following diagram of connections between the cycle's melodic, harmonic and tonal identities exists only as an abstraction, unless the ear catches onto such a simultaneity of time scales, the reality of time past and time future coexisting in time present:

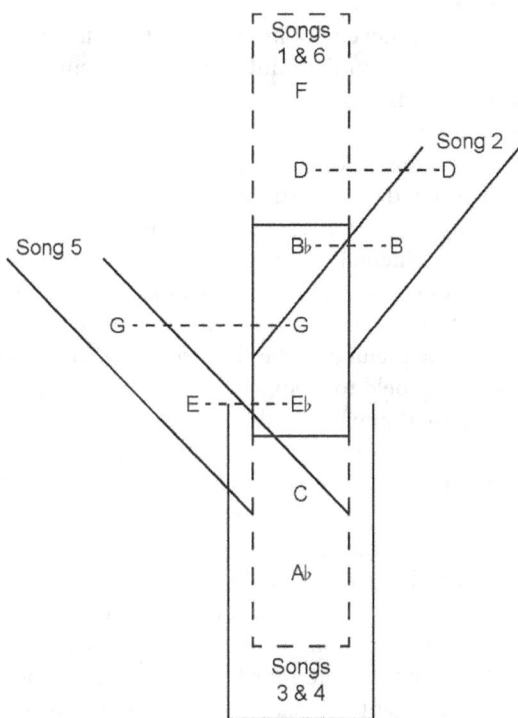

Figure 2.1 An die ferne Geliebte tonal scheme

Jeitteles's poet moves apparently effortlessly between here and there, then and now, to the confusion of any settled narrative in his cycle. In the second poem, the poet says he longs to be there in the peaceful valley, but also that nothing would draw him from here, if only the beloved were with him. In the third song the poet speaks of the autumnal bushes around him, but in the fifth song of the return of Spring. He may indeed have sat on his hill through the seasons, still watching for the beloved, or in one moment of longing be telling of a whole series of past experiences that are now brought together by memory. In the sixth and final poem the unity of the whole is projected forwards to the imagined performance of the beloved, who in one time and one place will succeed in singing back what she has heard. The reference to the beloved singing as the final rays of twilight disappear behind the mountain tops indicates that it is such a moment of experience that makes or breaks connections. For as much as the poet speaks of circling movements, streams that flow towards the beloved only to be sent back, as in the third verse of the fourth poem, the listener needs to grasp a specific shape from the poet's feelings in order to respond. Jeitteles creates potential for such a shape in the implied acceleration of movement from the mists of the second poem, to clouds, winds and streams in the third and fourth poems, to birds in the fifth poem. In as much as these act as carriers of sound, they climax in the beloved's song to the lute of the final poem.

Beethoven reflects this acceleration of movement in his cycle through the faster tempi of his third, fourth and fifth songs, also in the degree of rhythmic activity injected into the songs' melodic textures. Each of these songs offers heightened strings of alternating thirds, as though the third-related patterns of the first two songs were now breaking nearer to the musical surface. There is even a recasting of the cycle's falling third as a cuckoo call in the prelude to the fifth song. Yet the cuckoo call also suggests melody being held to a point of stasis. One can see a similar 'up and down on one spot' impulse in the way Beethoven injects rests into the melody of his third song, so giving greater prominence to the pedal points that sound through from the piano textures. The E♭ that marked the transition from the second to the third song rings on through much of the third song's piano textures, to remerge at the point of transition to the fourth song. The blurring of the boundaries between the third and fourth songs, their similar tonal and motivic character, becomes associated with this obsessive sounding of E♭ across both songs. The insistent dominant pedals in the third and fourth songs help reorientate the cycle from an emphasis on G, at the passage into the second song, to a heightened emphasis on E♭. Both of the pitches of the G-E♭ interval continue to act as sonorous presences that can inflect the cycle as a whole. An oscillation back to G emerges with the unison bell strokes at the point of transition to the fifth song, a unison that recalls the voice's monotonous insistence on G that accompanied the C major of the second verse of the second song.

The analogy with bell-strokes in the transition to the fifth song, an analogy intensified by the syncopation between the right and left hands of the piano, serves to underline the sense that the G-Eb pitches sound into space in defiance of the need for connections through time. They offer a presence that persists like images in 'the vast and boundless chamber' of memory, as Augustine puts it (St Augustine, 1993, 37). Yet such a sense of presence is not in itself sufficient for the task of singing back. If one were to stop the cycle before the sixth song, the blurring of the boundaries between songs would make the recalling of actual detail, of singable melody, almost impossible, since one detail blurs into another. How then can the beloved respond to the poet's call in the final poem to sing back what he has sung? The pause at the words 'Und du singst' (And you sing) in the third verse of Beethoven's setting of the sixth poem indicates a genuine crisis of memory. The sixth poem's second verse is set in declamatory fashion, the first time in the cycle that song-like melody is replaced with recitative-like phrases. Yet the pause for 'Und du singst' is succeeded by a stable and eloquent eight-bar statement, an arch that confirms the ease and self-sufficiency of melodic flight. The lean to the subdominant at the beginning of this arch is counterbalanced by the pull to the dominant of the fifth and sixth bars, to give an immediate sense of tonal equilibrium unusual in the cycle. The filled out piano textures also signal a contrast to the fragmentation of previous songs. This is a melody with supporting accompaniment, rather than a string of intervallic thirds, even though aspects of the G-Eb emphasis might still be detected, particularly in the use of G as the resting-point for the arch (see Example 2.18).

The other aspect that contributes to the sense of lyrical fulfilment at this moment of potential crisis is that this melodic arch is an exact replica of the first verse of the sixth song, which is itself almost an exact replica of the song's eight bars of piano preluding. Unlike the second, third, fourth and fifth songs of the cycle, the sixth song is provided with its own introduction and is not subject to a process of transition. The fifth song is brought to a steady close in bars 256–257 as the piano echoes the voice's final cadence, whilst the octave C added to the end of bar 257 can be heard as a straightforward upbeat to the beginning of the sixth song's melody in bar 258. If this single pitch is heard as a link, it is so only in the sense of clearing the throat for the full-voiced melody to follow; it can be heard as an 'all together now' signal, as before a moment of refrain in strophic song. And indeed this sixth song does not need a

Example 2.18 Beethoven *An die ferne Geliebte*, bars 283–292

transition to link it to the cycle as a whole because it offers an uncannily close memory of the melody with which the cycle opened. Example 2.18 recasts the eight-bar strophe of the first song, through melodically filling out the thirds that turned the original line into a string of sighs. One might say that the need for sighs disappears under the fulfilment of the beloved's response. Yet more specifically than that, Beethoven suggests how the beloved sings back the cycle's first melodic shape through the veil of what she has heard since. The melodic emphasis on C at the opening of this new melodic version carries forwards from the melodic and harmonic context of the previous fifth song, whilst the harmonic lean to A♭ reflects the key of the third and fourth songs.

From this viewpoint, the sixth song of Beethoven's cycle can be said to celebrate not just the success of communion with a distant beloved, but also the power of the lyric impulse to allow the past to be redeemed by the present:

> What might have been and what has been
> Point to one end, which is always present.
>   ('Burnt Norton')

The strophic repetitions of the one melodic arch, from the sixth song's first and third verses, underline how the cycle pulls into the present. A further repetition is indicated through a piano link at the end of the third verse, in bars 292–293, to indicate a sense of 'and so on, and so on'. From this invitation to further repetition, Beethoven draws out a return to the opening melody of the cycle as first presented, except that it is not so much a return as a picking up of the first song's strophic repetitions as though they had never left off. The strophic repetitions of the sixth song's new melody (Example 2.18) flow into the strophic repetitions of the original version, as though the two melodic versions were interchangeable because both feed from and into the one melodic spiral. In the first song the expansion and contraction of melody focussed on the building block of the intervallic third, the poet's sigh. In the sixth song the release of melodic variations from bar 305 creates a much more expansive impetus, one that significantly overflows the original eight-bar song shape. Yet the manner of the final cadence teases the ear with the notion that the spiral might still contract to one point, to the inversion of the G-E♭ interval that set the cycle in motion in the first place:

Example 2.19 Beethoven *An die ferne Geliebte*, bars 341–342

In many senses, in its claims upon the listener's memory, Beethoven's song-cycle behaves like a single strophic song (Boettcher, 1974, 67). It opens and closes upon one point, at the level of the strophe, at the level of the whole, with the knowledge that such a singleness of focus gives a measure to any expansions in time and space. The poet sits on the hill weaving his reverie, the beloved sits with her lute at twilight recalling what she has heard. Both processes are united as emanating from a basic impulse, a sigh. Beethoven's setting draws on techniques of harmonic and tonal projection to make the poet's sighs seem to extend beyond the boundaries of song, whilst the beloved picks them up as still being song. The composer's testing extends much further than the community of poets that his 'distant beloved' songs brought him into contact with. However, as this chapter has sought to demonstrate, even his song-cycle still belongs firmly within the musical, poetic and aesthetic contexts of the lyric. For all the cycle's exciting implications for modes of instrumental composition, *An die ferne Geliebte* remains Beethoven's most eloquent tribute to the distinctive power of strophic song.

References

Boettcher, Hans. *Beethoven als Liederkomponist*. Augsburg, Germany: Sändig, 1974.

Brun, Friederike. *Gedichte*. Zurich, Switzerland: Orell, Gessner, Füssli und compagnie, 1795.

Bürger, Gottfried August. *Gedichte*. Volume 1. Göttingen, Germany: Dieterich, 1789.

Chamberlain, Timothy J. (ed.). *Eighteenth Century German Criticism*. New York: Continuum, 1992.

Chambers English Dictionary. Cambridge: Cambridge University Press, 1988.

Cooper, Barry. *Beethoven and the Creative Process*. Oxford: Clarendon Press, 1990.

Cooper, Barry (ed.). *The Beethoven Compendium*. London: Thames and Hudson, 1996.

Eliot, T.S. *Four Quartets*. London: Faber & Faber Limited, 1968.

Friedlaender, Max. Goethes Gedichte in der Musik. *Goethe-Jahrbuch* XVII, 1896: 176–194.

Goethe, Johann Wolfgang von. *Selected Poems*, ed. Christopher Middleton. Princeton, NJ: Princeton University Press, 1994.

Hamburger, Michael (ed.). *Beethoven: Letters, Journals and Conversations*. London: Thames and Hudson, 1951.

Johnson, Douglas. 1794–1795: Decisive Years in Beethoven's Early Development. In *Beethoven Studies 3*, ed. Alan Tyson, 22–24. Cambridge: Cambridge University Press, 1982.

Matthisson, Friedrich von. *Gedichte*. Zurich, Switzerland: Orell, Gessner, Füssli und compagnie, 1815.

Reid, Paul. *The Beethoven Song Companion*. Manchester: Manchester University Press, 2007.

Reissig, Christian Ludwig. *Blümchen der Einsamkeit*. Vienna, Austria: Johann Baptist Wallishausser, 1809.

Schiller, Friedrich. *On the Aesthetic Education of Man*, ed. and tr. Elizabeth M. Wilkinson and L.A. Willoughby. Oxford: Clarendon Press, 1967.

Schiller, Friedrich. *Sämtliche Werke*. Volume 5, ed. Jost Perfahl. Munich, Germany: Winkler Verlag, 1968.

Schiller, Friedrich. *Über naïve und sentimentalische Dichtung*. Stuttgart, Germany: Reclam, 1993.

Schwab, Heinrich W. *Sangbarkeit, Popularität und Kunstlied: Studien zu Lied und Liedäs-thetik der mittleren Goethezeit 1770–1814*. Regensburg: Gustav Bosse, 1965.

Siegel, Linda (ed. and tr.). *Music in German Romantic Literature*. Novato, CA: Elra Publications, 1983.

Spitzer, Michael. *Music as Philosophy: Adorno and Beethoven's Late Style*. Bloomington and Indianapolis: Indiana University Press, 2006.

St Augustine. *Confessions*, ed. Justin Lovill, tr. J.G. Pilkington. London: Folio Society, 1993.

Stein, Jack. *Poem and Music in the German Lied from Gluck to Hugo Wolf*. Cambridge, MA: Harvard University Press, 1971.

Sternfeld, Frederick. *Goethe and Music: A List of Parodies*. New York: New York Public Library, 1954.

Stoljar, Margaret Mahony. *Poetry and Song in Late Eighteenth-Century Germany*. London: Croom Helm, 1985.

Tyson, Alan (ed.). *Beethoven Studies*. New York: W.W. Norton, 1973.

3 The retelling of lyric

Beethoven's Ninth Symphony

The line of song engagement described in Chapter 2 is rather different from what some Beethoven enthusiasts might expect. The prevalence of strophic forms, implying respect for immediate poetic boundaries, sits strangely with the image of Beethoven as a Behemoth who transcends all limits, the image from Grillparzer with which this book began. The composer who partners Reissig's 'Songs of Loneliness' with such intimate sensitivity might seem miles away from the revolutionary symphonist. One might conclude from this that the songs belong in a context of occasional composition, rather than with the main body of Beethoven's oeuvre (Dahlhaus, 1991, 3). But the composer also offers, as this chapter will seek to show, a line of songs that fits more easily with his revolutionary associations, songs that are more obviously innovative – both in their musical form and in how they relate to poetic modes of address.

As with Goethe, one can identify two opposing strands in Beethoven's poetic sensibility. Fairley talks of Goethe's poetry as having a Faustian and a non-Faustian aspect. The first speaks in great 'gusts of emotion' as though from a 'stormy vein' (Fairley, 1963, 105); the second, as seen most in his short poems, comes from 'watching and waiting, from submission, from reserve, from understatement' (Fairley, 1963, 107). It is part of the supreme range of Goethe's lyricism that one strand can seem to 'supplement or elucidate or correct the other' (Fairley, 1963, 110). This process of cross referral challenges how one views the lyric. For the lyric tends to be defined by its immediacy, by its qualities as 'first nature' (Lukács, 1971, 62). Staiger even says that 'lyric poetry does not overcome anything' and offers no test of strength. Rather it concerns an outpouring of feeling, 'the joy of one moment of inspiration' (Staiger, 1991, 96). Lyricists seek to tell of this feeling, but once they can reflect on the mood and give it a name, 'the *lied* is over' (Staiger, 1991, 91). Goethe himself speaks, in a letter to Schiller of April 1801, of the importance of unconsciousness in poetic creation (Herzfeld, 1957, 311), yet for him this state emerges at its most powerful when blended with consciousness; he sees consciousness and unconsciousness working together as the 'warp and weft' of poetry (Herzfeld, 1957, 537). With *Faust* he talks of seeking to distil what is in him again and again (Herzfeld, 1957, 538). Hence the poet offers not so much a telling of his feeling, as apparently endless cycles of retelling.

Benedetto Croce saw Part 2 of *Faust* as offering 'a kind of loosely assembled bouquet of reminiscences, an anthology of fine lyrical passages' (Gray, 1967, 160). They only come into focus as a listener responds to them as song. Goethe even offers a specific lesson in song creation in an exchange between Faust and Helen in Act 3 of Part 2:

Faust: If you already like the way our peoples speak.
I'm sure their singing will delight you too,
will fully satisfy both ear and mind.
Delay is dangerous – let's practice it at once;
responses are what tempt us to employ it.
Helen: Then tell me how I too can learn the art.
Faust: It's simple: let the words well from your heart.
And when your soul is filled with yearning's flame,
you look around and ask
Helen: who feels the same.

(Goethe, 1984, 236–237)

This lesson points up the significance of the songs heard throughout *Faust*. The involvement of Helen, a godlike figure whom Schiller describes as uniting art and nature (Schiller, 1967, 109), promises to give new lustre to the experience of the lyric, though the lesson has to work with the reality of song if it is not to seem superfluous or even hubristic. The listener is encouraged to think back to the actual songs of Gretchen to see if they match up to such heightened expectations. And indeed, in Fairley's view, it is songs that bring *Faust* to completion, songs that step outside the immediate narrative to invoke Goethe's lyric power as a whole (Fairley, 1963, 119). At the point where the drama is nearing conclusion, Gretchen's 'Neige, neige, / Du Ohnegleiche' returns to the rhythms of her song 'Ach neige, / Du Schmerzenreiche' from Part 1, a song which is itself based on the well-known Latin hymn 'Stabat Mater' (Sternfeld, 1954, 82–83). Goethe identifies such simultaneity of forwards and backwards movements with the epic, in contrast to the steady forwards movement of drama (Herzfeld, 1957, 254). But taking *Faust*'s final scene as a whole – its winding progress among mountain gorges – its manner comes closest of all perhaps to the circularity of the lyric, as rounds of hymnic repetition seek to capture the glory of one evanescent moment. Staiger suggests Goethe is famous for continually mixing characteristics of the lyric, epic, and dramatic (Staiger, 1991, 136). But without the example of *Faust*, its particular way of celebrating lyric song as a final test and solution, the creative role of the lyric might be in danger of slipping past unmarked. As is borne out by the correspondence between Schiller and Goethe, the epic and dramatic are much easier to define (Staiger, 1991, 72). Goethe says there should always be something 'unreasonable' about the detail of a lyric; it becomes 'reasonable' only as a whole (Goethe, 1998, 16). And it is this sense of perspective on the totality of the lyric impulse that Goethe conveys so eloquently in the conclusion of *Faust*, as in the ritual of the final scene, dramatic and epic elements fall away to reveal a lyrical essence – or perhaps a metaphorical silence where the presence of the lyric can be intuited.

If one continues to follow Grillparzer in linking Beethoven to Goethe, then the elusiveness of the lyric impulse within the composer's creative profile might seem quite appropriate. As with Goethe's poetry, many of Beethoven's songs offer themselves as heady mixtures of all three poetic modes: lyric, epic and dramatic. Pursuing the Goethe comparison one step further, one might ask whether the composer's biggest generic mixture – the Ninth Symphony – might not be taken, like *Faust*, as his supreme vehicle for capturing the significance of lyric song. In the Ninth's finale, as in the scene between Helen and Faust, there is an explicit call for individual and communal voices to be brought together in song. As the baritone soloist declares 'Friends, not these tones, but let us sing something more pleasant', Beethoven – like Goethe – evokes a power coming from somewhere else, even from outside the work. William Kinderman emphasises the composer's sympathy with the idealising effect of the words of Schiller's poem (Kinderman, 1995, 13), words which break in after the baritone's urgent appeal. As John Reid has pointed out, Beethoven pored over the possibility of setting the words of Schiller's ode for much of his composing life (Reid, 2007, 194). But interestingly enough the melody Beethoven offers for these words in the Ninth's finale comes from an equally long obsession with the poet Bürger. As referred to in Chapter 2, the tune for the 'Ode to Joy' draws on Beethoven's setting of Bürger's *Gegenliebe*, with its simple *Tanzlied* associations. Like Goethe, Beethoven can be said to be referencing his own history of involvement with the lyric as a means of bringing his grand work to conclusion. Through song Beethoven shows how the non-symphonic can jostle shoulders with the symphonic and even invade each other's territory, just as Goethe plays with Faustian and non-Faustian poetry in *Faust*.

As will be seen, there are specific compositional processes in the Ninth Symphony that link it to song. But the Ninth's finale can also be viewed more generally as a sign that for Beethoven the role of the lyric need not be dwarfed by the incursion of even the most extreme dramatic and epic elements. Such a message emanates from the composer's 1815 setting of Tiedge's *An die Hoffnung*, a hugely challenging song that was composed on the brink of his last period. This was Beethoven's second attempt to do justice to Tiedge's outcry to hope, which in referencing the heights and depths of suffering seems to transcend what any individual might experience. The poet offers a universal reflection on the intermingling of earthly and heavenly perspectives. As Reid discusses, the poem is one canto within Tiedge's six-canto 'lyric-didactic poem' *Urania: Über Gott, Unsterblichkeit und Freiheit*, a larger context which affects the intimacy of the poem (Reid, 2007, 61–62). Hope is addressed directly as 'Du' as befits the genre of the ode, but the poet speaks of himself in the third person as 'Der Dulder' (the sufferer). In referring to 'the dream of life' he seems to be ranging over all times and places; in speaking of 'versunkne Urnen' (buried urns) and 'Das Leuchten eines Wolkensaumes' (the light from the cloud's fringe), the poet could be looking back in memory or imagining the future. Yet the vividness of such imagery still points to the effect of moments of feeling, moments in which distinctions of future, past and present become overtaken by the intensity of lyric experience.

In his first setting of *An die Hoffnung*, from the period 1804–1805, Beethoven acknowledged the lyric basis of Tiedge's poem by keeping an exact pattern of strophic repetition for all three verses. The melodic appoggiatura figure at the cadence in bar 7 marks out the poetic rhymes that help contain the complexity of the ode's metrical makeup; the rising appoggiatura of 'feierst' in bar 7 is matched by the fall of 'verschleierst' in bar 9, even though the poem's second line is a metrical foot shorter than the first. A similar rise and fall reoccurs to mark the rhyme of 'emporgehoben' and 'oben' in bars 17 and 19, and again in bars 26 and 28 as Beethoven expands the verse with a large-scale repetition of the poetic text. The musical phrases contract and expand seemingly at will, but as with the poem a rhyming function helps maintain the level of lyric intensity. The song's prelude and postlude both close by referring to the Ab-G appoggiatura figure of bars 7 and 9, so that even the piano's passages of harp-like figuration are drawn into the rhyming function.

Interestingly, when Beethoven came to reset *An die Hoffnung* in 1815, the harp-like figuration seems to have been the main element to stay in his compositional imagination. Indeed, it dominates much of the textural and melodic shaping of the recomposed first verse. Triplet figures spill over from the preludial passage of bars 27 to 28; they infect not only the accompanying textures that follow but also the vocal line. The twists and turns of the melodic triplets in bars 32–33 seem instrumental rather than vocal in character, designed to generate energy for the accelerating rises and falls that mark the subsequent passage. Here the rhymes of 'emporge-hoben' (bar 35) and 'oben' (bar 36) are brought out by extremes of registral ascent followed by immediate descents. The sighing steps of tone or semitone of Beethoven's first setting are replaced by rise and falls across the compass of an octave. The voice takes up the C to C melodic sweep of the two bars of piano prelude with its D to D sweep (bars 29–30), followed by E to E (bars 35–36), then rising to G to G (bars 36–37).

The song's vocal line almost breaks under such extremes. As a performer one might be tempted to deliver the phrases as fragments of declamation, in the style of the passage of recitative which Beethoven appends to this second setting. Yet within each vocal phrase Beethoven inserts melismas that indicate a legato or gliding style of presentation. These melismas become particularly prominent with the slurring articulation of the repeated phrase 'seine Tränen zählt' (counts his tears). In bar 37 the melisma on 'Trä' encompasses a sixth, then expands to a seventh in bar 42 which is almost the full scope of the vocal line's characteristic octave sweeps. From that point the syllable is accompanied by falling semitones, in bars 43 and 44, as though the vocal line were now being allowed to contract to a more usual style of expression; the phrase resolves with an echo of the first setting's cadential sigh on 'zählt' in bar 45. Thus for all its melodic rises and falls the verse ends by suggesting a process of lyric containment. The large-scale musical and poetic repeat of the song's first verse from the end of bar 71 offers a vital opportunity for the listener to test the overall effect of the verse, whether its exaggerated shapes can indeed resolve into a sense of single focus as one would expect of a lyric strophe. The performance instruction *espressivo*, given to the piano and voice's preparatory sighing figures in bars 70 and 71, confirms that what is at stake here is the mode of address – whether the following vocal sweeps and flourishes can be sung as lyric or whether they must be declaimed as drama.

The question whether lyric or drama should predominate in Beethoven's second setting of *An die Hoffnung* is heightened by the episodes that are inserted into the song's overall structure of repetition. The introductory section to the first verse presents a decidedly dramatic context for the song as a whole. Apart from the voice's clear reference to recitative-like fragmentation, the piano evokes orchestral style scene-painting, as might be suitable for a gloomy Faust in his study or Florestan in his dungeon. It is almost inevitable that this introduction invites comparison with the beginning of Act 2 of Beethoven's opera *Fidelio*. Apart from the closeness in the style and content of the vocal phrases – the urgent recitative that pits doubt against faithful submission to God – the piano textures closely resemble the winding chromaticism of the seven-bar orchestral introduction to Florestan's first *Adagio cantabile* aria section. Both passages outline a tertiary modulation – E to A♭ in the case of the opera, B♭ to G in the song introduction – that evokes a change of mood from a world of despair to an imagined new beginning. Except that in the song, echoes of the introduction continue to invade the following section. The vocal line of the introduction hovers around three pitches, C-C#/D♭-D, and taken in reverse order these become a kind of tag within the song's subsequent verse. Having marked the link into the change of tempo to *Larghetto* for the first verse (bars 22–27), they appear in passing during the second bar of the *Larghetto*'s prelude (bar 28) and more emphatically as a way of highlighting 'Gram' (sorrow) in bar 31. Most significantly, they appear in connection with the repetitions of 'Tränen zählt' in bar 38 and in bars 42–45, and with the poetic notion of an angel counting the sufferer's tears. What might be seen as melodically passing is turned into a summary; the impact of the song's dramatic contrasts can be set against this supreme attention to detail which characterises the lyric.

Beethoven's attention to detail continues even with the return of the dramatic style of the introduction for his setting of the poem's second and third stanzas. A quasi-orchestral mode of punctuation is indicated by the pauses within the piano's linking passage from bar 46, and by the dramatic unisons that break into bars 58 and 62. The voice's sweeping rise and fall in bars 60–61 is reminiscent of the first verse, but the melodic glue seems to have disappeared – until the subsequent D-C#-C descent on 'Tagen' (bar 62) offers a timely echo. As the poem refers to the last rays of a dying sun, Beethoven insinuates this tag of memory. The three pitches in bar 62 anticipate the melodic and harmonic steps, in bars 69 to 71, that serve as a link to the return of the first verse and the tonic G in bar 72. But before such containment, Beethoven stretches the bounds of the song one stage further. The extra chromatic slip from C to B, emphasised in bar 63 as a tonal step to B major, ushers in a musical no-man's-land. In terms of the poem, Tiedge envisages a kind of death at this point as the sun's rays sink below the horizon. Musically Beethoven dares to offer a free-floating vocal line that exceeds the previous sweep of an octave, rising to almost two octaves from its lowest point on B in bar 63 in one dizzying ascent to its highest point of A in bar 69. There is an impression of epic dimensions introduced by this passage, in the sense that at the moment of being pulled back by a tag of memory, in bar 62, the horizon shifts to take in much bigger vistas. In the way that Adorno believes is typical of the late period, Beethoven sets up the parameters of genre only to threaten to break them apart (Adorno, 1998, 191–192). The lyric's distinctive focus on detail – in the words of Tiedge, the detail that comes from observing the 'the light from the cloud's fringe' – is pitted against epic proportions where such detail is in danger of being swamped or even lost in what Adorno calls 'artistically contrived fissures' in the music. In Adorno's opinion, in late Beethoven there is no midway, 'no balancing, no homoeostasis, no mediation of any sort as a middle term between the extremes, but, as in Hegel, only a mediation passing through the extremes' (Adorno, 1998, 191). It is as though the musical gulfs can only be bridged in the moment of experiencing them, not in terms that can be abstracted from the experience. In this sense the power of the singing voice to hold the line, to transfer with apparent ease between lyric detail and epic sweep in the moment of performance, becomes what makes the song. When the repeat of the first verse is introduced at the end of bar 71, listeners have to decide whether they are persuaded by the singer to hear all the surrounding contrasts as colours that come and go at the whim of the lyricist – or whether, like Boettcher, they simply hear an aria manqué (Boettcher, 1974, 25).

Beethoven's late setting of *An die Hoffnung* tests the stamina of performers as well as the receptivity of listeners to the limit. It would be difficult to find another Beethoven song that plays so provocatively and exhaustingly with the performers' resources. But the aesthetic challenge that underlies it – of teasing out the lyric from elements of the epic and dramatic – appears in one of the composer's very first songs. The setting of Hölty's *Klage*, which comes from Beethoven's pre-Vienna years, offers an almost experimental approach to song. Barry Cooper claims this song shows the composer 50 years ahead of his time (Cooper, 2000, 38), but one might say that no one has ever caught up with it. The first verse is notable for its melodic poise which seems to capture the poem's image of moonlight circling through leaves. It is this quality of inviolate calm that probably led to it being chosen for the hero to sing in a salon scene from the BBC's production of George Eliot's *Daniel Deronda*, though interestingly Daniel performs only the first verse – as though it were a little song complete in itself. The interweaving of the piano and voice parts, as they hover over the melodic mediant, creates a delicate balance between openness and closure. It draws attention to the sighing shapes of the singer's breath while also carrying them forwards to the resolution on the melodic and harmonic tonic at the end of the strophe. Such a process of linking breath to the creation of periodic melody draws the listener into the immediacy of singing; a circle of moonlight becomes associated with a circle of melody. Even Beethoven's unusually lengthy instructions to the singer hint at a special act of evocation: 'Throughout the notes must be legato, and as far as possible sustained and joined together' (Reid, 2007, 194).

One might imagine that the weaving of such melodic threads would continue into the second and third verses of the song as, according to the poem, moonlight recurs to guide the poet through the contrasting scenes of his life, from the leafy forest, to the empty chamber, to the dark tombstone:

Dein Silber schien
Durch Eichengrün,
Das Kühlung gab,
Auf mich herab,
O Mond, und lachte Ruh'
Mir frohem Knaben zu.

Wenn jetzt dein Licht
Durchs Fenster bricht,
Lacht's keine Ruh'
Mir Jüngling zu,
Sieht's meine Wange blass,
Meine Auge Tränennass.

Bald, lieber Freund,
Ach bald bescheint
Dein Silberschein
Den Leichenstein,
Der meine Asche birgt,
Des Jünglings Asche birgt.
(Hölty, 1783, 100)

[Your silvery light shone down on me,
Through the cool of the green oak leaves,
O moon, smiling peace
Onto the happy boy.

When now your light breaks through the window,
It no longer smiles peace onto the youth,
It sees the ashen cheeks,
My eyes wet with tears.

Soon, dear friend, ah soon will shine
Your silvery light onto the tombstone,
That hides my ashes,
That hides the youth's ashes.]
(Author's translation)

When Schubert came to set this poem he introduced increasingly chromatic harmonies from the beginning of the second verse while retaining the smoothly rocking melody of the first stanza. Even in the third verse – where the rise in the vocal register, the tonal shift from F major to D minor and the sound of tolling bells within the piano texture all indicate an increase in dramatic tension – the vocal line holds its rhythmic poise. The song moves from light to dark, but within a single melodic stream of rhyming phrases. Beethoven hints at a similar mid-flow change of colour by inserting minor mode inflexions into the song's piano interlude in bars 14–15. Such hints increase the shock when the melodic thread is actually broken at the beginning of the second verse. At bar 16 the change of mode is accompanied by a change of tempo – from *Langsam und sanft* to *Sehr langsam und traurig* – and even by a change of style. Melodic poise is replaced by exaggerated rise and falls and an *agitato* accompanying texture. Beethoven is emphasising the narrative aspect of Hölty's poem as though the boy of the first verse and the youth of the second have been split apart by the nature of life's experiences. The continuity provided by the cycles of the moon is shown to break under the impact of human change and tragedy. Schiller refers to the 'independence of parts' as characteristic of the epic (Staiger, 1991, 116). Beethoven's second verse might indeed be viewed as an independent episode, rather than a lyric strophe. The second verse is left hanging on an imperfect cadence in bar 23, with a dominant pedal tolling through most of the third verse to suggest the pull to tonal resolution as a symbol of the relentlessness of death. Beethoven makes full play of the drama of musical closure, but the actual melodic style of this third verse is not declamatory. The circling vocal phrases from bar 24 reintroduce the first verse's hovering on the melodic mediant, as though the piano's repeated Bs at the close of the second verse might offer a door back to the past, repeated Bs having figured prominently in the link from the first to the second verse. The third verse offers no literal return to the melodic arches of the song's opening, but there are still echoes of the basic heartbeat or breath-shapes from which that melody sprang. Indeed both the second and third verses of Beethoven's setting continue to hold to the steady two-bar phrasing of periodic melody. They hold a space in which the exemplary poise of the song's first verse can be remembered. The slowing of the tempo for the song's second verse suggests something of this reluctance to move forward. Once the thread of the first verse's melody is broken, the ensuing epic and dramatic contrasts indicate the vacuum where the melody has been. One might call this a new way of celebrating strophic song, of paying tribute to the power of a lyric moment. The melody of the first verse is not repeated, once it is gone it is gone. But in the continued chiming of two-bar phrase shapes Beethoven prolongs the physical memory of the song and its patterns of breathing, so inviting the listener to continue to play the memory of the first verse in their heads.

So how should Beethoven's setting of *Klage* be categorised? It might be tempting to view it as a quasi-operatic *scena*, as a depiction of three equally vivid scenes. In terms of the definitions set out by Emil Staiger, if one experiences the song's threefold contrast as allowing it to reach its goal, then it should be characterised as a drama. If, on the other hand, the tripartite structure appears to exist for the sake of exploring depths of contrast, then the song should be characterised as epic (Staiger, 1991, 114). It is possible to view *Klage* in both these ways, but neither really does justice to the magnetism of Beethoven's setting. The power of the first verse, as demonstrated by its treatment in *Daniel Deronda*, is that it seems to exist in itself. The following contrasts can be heard to confirm such lyric self-containment, provided listeners continue to tune in to the immediacy of the singer's breath and the predictability of the question-and-answer phrasing. If heard in this lyric mode, then the narrative of the poet's despair can simultaneously be embraced as an extreme version of Shakespeare's cycle of the common ages of man in *As You Like It*. The cyclical nature of the moon can be understood to keep its sway over the lives of men, even if – in Beethoven's setting – it has to fight for prominence with the twists and turns of an individual fate. There is the potential for a precious sense of communality in this song's experiment with periodic melody, a communality that might be taken for granted in a more literal strophic setting.

It is notable that even in such an early song Beethoven reveals an instinct for mixing epic, lyric and dramatic modes to surprising effect. His testing of musical parameters – of melody, rhythm, phrase and stanza – is linked to a testing of basic aesthetic definitions, so that the listener is forced to rethink what terms such as lyric and dramatic might mean. One can hear such explorations continuing into the composer's setting of Matthisson's *Adelaide*, which was composed four years after *Klage* in the period 1794–1795. This song is recognised as one of Beethoven's masterpieces of song-writing, in particular for bringing the full resources of the instrumental sonata to the genre of the Viennese keyboard song. Yet its popularity is in danger of masking the significance of its delicate balancing act. In his critical essay on Matthisson's poetry Schiller says it presents an 'ever changing drama' (Schiller, 1968, 699), one that leaves the reader in danger of being 'erblendet' (blinded) rather than 'erquickt' (enlivened) (Schiller, 1968, 704). In *Adelaide*, the poet's Hölty-like journey from envisaging the shimmering blossoms of spring (verse 1) to petals on a grave (verse 4), is expanded to include scenes of alpine snow (verse 2)

and of waves roaring on a sea shore (verse 3). The poet offers his experience of Nature as a kaleidoscope of impressions, rather than as a single
moment stretched into timelessness:

> Einsam wandelt dein Freund im Frühlingsgarten,
> Mild vom lieblichen Zauberlicht umflossen,
> Das durch wankende Blütenzweige zittert,
> Adelaide!
>
> In der spiegelnden Fluth, im Schnee der Alpen,
> In der sinkenden Tages Goldgewölken,
> Im Gefilde der Sterne strahlt dein Bildnis,
> Adelaide!
>
> Abendlüftchen im zarten Laube flüstern,
> Silberglöckchen des Mais im Grase säuseln,
> Wellen rauschen und Nachtigallen flöten:
> Adelaide!
>
> Einst, o Wunder! entblüht auf meinem Grabe,
> Eine Blume der Asche meines Herzens;
> Deutlich schimmert auf jedem Purpurblättchen:
> Adelaide!
>
>   (Matthisson, 1912, 135–136)

[Your friend wanders lonely in the spring garden,
Surrounded by the soft wonders of magical light,
That shimmers through the swaying blossoms,
Adelaide!

In the mirror of the waves, in the snow of the alps,
In the gold-tinged clouds of the sinking day,
In the starry host shines your image,
Adelaide!

Evening breezes whisper through the tracery of leaves,
Silver bells of May-time tinkle in the grass,
Waves rustle and nightingales trill:
Adelaide!

One day, O miracle! There will bloom on my grave
A flower from my heart's ashes;

Clear on each purple petal will shine:
Adelaide!]
             (Author's translation)

Beethoven's setting of *Adelaide* is not entitled 'Lied' or even 'Gesang'. The song was published in 1797 as a 'cantata', as a way of introducing listeners to its multi-sectional nature. Beethoven highlights the poet's restlessness almost immediately by the improvisatory nature of his vocal line. The asymmetrical structure of three-two-three bar phrasing prevents a predictable swing of question-and-answer responses. In Matthisson's poem the sounding of the name 'Adelaide' acts as a steadying refrain at the end of each stanza. In Beethoven's setting, the C-B♭ appoggiatura which marks the first repetitions of the beloved's name in bars 15 and 17 refers back pitch-wise to the end of the song's first vocal phrase, in bar 8, and to the end of the verse in bar 13. However, the rhythmic variation in bars 8 and 13 prevents such rhymes from fully settling. The alternation between crotchet and quaver phrase-endings, between a steady and a snatched pattern of breathing, makes the poet's thoughts hard to catch. It is the piano textures that provide much of the sense of direction and purpose in the song, as though words were being left behind in the speed of emotional change. The two-bar figure that emerges in the piano in bar 13, as a link from the first to the second verse, recurs at regular intervals throughout the second verse; it is this that provides some sense of regular phrasing (see Example 3.1).

As has often been pointed out, Beethoven continues to vary the vocal treatment of the beloved's name throughout his setting. In the third verse, as though in response to the further spiral of instrumentally derived modulatory sequences, he changes the basic cadence of 'Adelaide' from a 'feminine' to a 'masculine' ending in bar 58. An urge to find dramatic resolution appears to overtake an impulse to sigh over echoes of the past, even if the tonal context at this point – G♭ major, the flat submediant – shows the resolution is only temporary. As in a dramatic sonata-form structure, the search for tonal closure is stretched from the immediate to the longer term. This 'masculine' cadence in the wrong key prepares the way for three more emphatic 'masculine' renderings of 'Adelaide' in the fourth and final verse, in bars 111, 152 and 171 – each emphasising arrival on the tonic B♭. The third cadence might seem appropriate to a fully dramatic operatic aria rather than song. Given such a climactic arrival-point the voice's final reference to 'Adelaide' in bars 177–179, complete with the C-B♭ melodic appoggiatura of bar 15, appears as an afterthought (see Example 3.2).

From maximum expansion, the vocal line contracts back towards where it started; a more intimate rendering of the single word re-emerges

Example 3.1 Beethoven *Adelaide*, bars 13–23

from the press of instrumentally driven sequences. It is interesting to compare this moment of vocal delivery with the way the beloved's name is treated at the beginning of the fourth verse. In bar 104, and in bar 145 where the section is repeated, the vocal articulation quite explicitly follows the promptings of the piano and its two-bar patterns of alternating dominant and tonic (see Example 3.3).

The verbal text at this point could in a sense be anything, any of the two-bar poetic phrases that are repeated through this final coda-like section, whether 'Deutlich schimmert' or 'Einst, o Wunder!'. Of course, the internal rhythm of the musical phrase would have to be adapted, just as it is adapted to fit 'Adelaide' after the piano's introduction of its motif

Example 3.2 Beethoven *Adelaide*, bars 177–181

Example 3.3 Beethoven *Adelaide*, bars 102–105

in bars 102 and 143. Throughout the fourth verse the piano tends to take the lead whilst the voice is made to fit in with its articulation. One sees this at the beginning of the verse in bar 72, where the phrase for 'Einst, o Wunder' comes in as an answer to the piano's previous two-bar motif. In contrast to this, the voice's final extra 'Adelaide' is allowed to linger – to find its own space, as it were, within the piano's dominant-tonic alternations.

Despite such contrasts in vocal delivery one would be unlikely to experience *Adelaide* as having a double ending; the drama of tonal resolution clearly predominates. However, the song's final echo acts as a reminder that this drama is still drawing on lyric elements – on the stretching and contracting of a single word, for example. The song's focus upon the detail of verbal articulation can seem blurred at times by the pure inventiveness of the instrumental writing, but there is one notable moment in the final verse where the rhythm of particular words seems to control the instrumental flow. The two-bar motivic figure for 'Deutlich schimmert' is introduced in bar 94 by the voice, not the piano, and is answered by another two-bar figure from the voice – 'auf jedem Purpurblättchen' – rather than by a piano motif. This seems the most straightforwardly song-like sequence in the whole of Beethoven's setting, a passage that rings on in the head once the large-scale drama is completed. As the poet attempts to summarise his experiences the vocal repetitions etch out the single phrase 'Clear on each purple petal will shine', so setting up the question 'what will shine' and the one word answer: 'Adelaide'.

If one revisits Bettina von Arnim's fanciful words on Beethoven's approach to song-writing, one notes she envisages the composer's enthusiasm for motivic development overriding all other impulses:

> Goethe's poems exercise great power over me not only by their content, but by their rhythm. His language is such that is stimulates me and puts me in a mood to compose, for, as if with the aid of spirits, it attains a higher order and contains the secret of harmony within it. So, from the focal point of enthusiasm, I must discharge melody in all directions. I pursue it, passionately catch up with it again, see it flee from me and vanish in the crowd of excitements; now I seize it with renewed passion, cannot bear to part with it, must multiply it in all its modulations in a quick ecstasy, and at the last moment I triumph over the first musical idea. You see, that's a symphony.
>
> (Hamburger, 1951, 88)

Bettina is here clearly describing a dramatic rather than a lyric process, one weighted towards thematic return and resolution. She calls the result a 'symphony', everything sounding together. This does not necessarily imply that Beethoven has moved beyond song, however. One might quote Johann Georg Sulzer on the kinship between a symphonic Allegro and a Pindaric ode; according to him, both move from the 'apparent disorder' of contrast and variation to the 'combining [of] all voices' in what comes to seem like a single melody (Baker and Christensen, 1995, 105). Sulzer insists vocally derived melody should emerge triumphant even in purely instrumental composition. He says the instrumental composer should imitate the utterance of a person ready to speak from extreme emotion, or should imagine a poem that provides a suitable sentiment, 'pathetic, fiery, or tender in nature' (Baker and Christensen, 1995, 96). For Sulzer song and symphony feed off each other. Yet bringing symphonic impulses into song still implies a provocative stretching of generic boundaries. In Bettina's fantasy Beethoven's song-writing seems in danger of leaving the words behind, unless the return to 'the first musical idea' is heard to re-invoke the moment when poetic rhythms first turn into melody. In *Adelaide*, the unexpected afterword – 'Adelaide' – is just such an evocation; it is as though Beethoven were retelling how the song arose from the rhythmic impetus of a single word. Having experienced the instrumentally driven power of variation and modulation, listeners are directed back to its potential origins in the detail of verbal inflexion. They are invited to think back and adjust what they have heard; the song may still be experienced as drama, but drama as emanating from a lyric impulse.

Drama encompassing lyric is by nature an easier process to envisage than lyric encompassing drama. Peter Szondi points out how Friedrich Schlegel, Beethoven's near contemporary, believed the novelising tone of the epic offered the greatest potential for dissolving generic boundaries (Szondi, 1986, 85–89). In treating the different poetic genres as adjectives rather than nouns he sought a new fluidity between them (Szondi, 1986, 80), though his preoccupation with the novel still gave the epic precedence within his aesthetic schema. If one were to seek to summarise Beethoven's aesthetic predisposition one would probably focus on the dramatic; as many have pointed out, a search for resolution figures prominently in his compositional processes. Yet these two early songs, *Klage* and *Adelaide*, challenge such generalisations. Their mixtures almost defy categorisation; the balance of generic expectations can only be decided by the experience of the song itself, by the moment of performance or of hearing. In this, Beethoven's songs can once again be compared to aspects of Goethe's poetry. When speaking of his ballads, Goethe says their flight comes from performers continuing to re-mix the elements of the epic, lyric and drama, as they respond to the 'Ur-Ei' (source egg) created by the poet (Goethe, 1887–1912, 223). None of the three poetic modes can be given preeminence *a priori*. Goethe treats ballads as a particular category within song, a place of multiple voices and multiple dimensions. But even when speaking of what one might call the lyric proper, Goethe says it would be good for the poet to be two people – one to experience and one to describe the experience (Herzfeld, 1957, 105). From such a point of view, there can be no such thing as a pure lyric; with poetic song there is always an element of epic, of recounting something that is happening elsewhere. But Goethe implies that these two aspects, experience and the observation of experience, can be teased out as voices; and if they are voiced then they can be made to engage in counterpoint with one another.

Goethe's tiny poem *Wonne der Wehmut* gives perhaps the clearest exposition of his belief both in the primacy of the lyric moment and in the need for such moments to be told. The poem is uncompromisingly intimate, as though intended for private rather than public edification.

Although written around 1775, the poem was not published until 1789. The poet's insistence that the world should be seen through tears suggests an almost wilful dulling of the outward senses as time and space are contracted into the measure of a tear drop:

> Trocknet nicht, trocknet nicht,
> Thränen der ewigen Liebe!
> Ach! nur dem halbgetrockneten Auge
> Wie öde, wie tot die Welt ihm erscheint!
> Trocknet nicht, trocknet nicht,
> Thränen unglücklicher Liebe!
>
> (Goethe, 1827, 108)

> [Do not dry, do not dry,
> The tears of eternal love!
> Ah, only to tears that are half-dried
> How empty, how dead the world seems!
> Do not dry, do not dry,
> Tears of unhappy love!]
>
> (Author's translation)

The amount of repetition within the poem underlines the singlemindedness of its message. The poem's metrical makeup – its alternation of dactyls and trochees, its irregular line-lengths – disrupts a smooth sense of time unfolding. Instead the ear is drawn to the sounds set off by the immediate repetition of words and syllables, beginning with the four-times repeated 'Trocknet nicht'. This dactyl is split into a series of internal resonances by the explosion of 'ck' followed by 'net' and 'nicht'. The hiccough of 'ck', like the gulp that comes with tears, brings time almost to a standstill as though one were waiting for a single tear to drop. As the two words are repeated, 'Tr' marks the beginning of the next tear forming, and 'nicht' the point where after hovering it finally falls. The third tear, suggested by the 'Thr' of 'Thränen' at the start of the second line, turns into something more like a stream, however. The long vowel sounds of 'ewigen' and 'Liebe' create an immediate sense of release, so preparing for the impetus of 'Ach' and the momentum of the poem's longer third and fourth lines. There is no reference to events in the external world, but Goethe succeeds in suggesting an internal drama of holding and releasing emotion that can be mapped externally in the changing flow of tears. There is even a point of resolution as the substitution of 'unglücklicher

Liebe' for 'ewigen Liebe' in the poem's final line draws the ear back to the hiccough ('ck') of the single tear.

It is a defining aspect of the lyric to turn the inside outwards, but in *Wonne der Wehmut* Goethe not only does this but demonstrates how it might be done. The shape of a present moment, as it forms and as it passes, is caught through sound events that emanate from the experience of living those moments. The tear is both visual, and thus open for an observer to measure and count, and aural in responding to an inner resonance where time no longer seems to matter. As Goethe says in conversations with Eckermann:

> Always hold fast to the present. Every situation, indeed every moment, is of infinite value, for it is the representation of a whole eternity.
>
> (Goethe, 1966, 124)

One might say that in *Wonne der Wehmut* the poet confronts such a paradox head on, through the way he creates a simultaneity of perspective that allows the small to be heard as big. Composers certainly responded to this poem as far more than a paean to romantic sensibility. Zelter's setting of 1807 is unusually complex and declamatory in its rhythms, creating long winding melodic arches for both the voice and the keyboard. Schubert, like Reichardt, creates a more immediately satisfying melodic pattern out of the poet's refrain 'Trocknet nicht', though he introduces a string of harmonic excursions to disturb the evenness of his melodic line. Beethoven's setting also contains clear melodic shaping, but the drama that begins to unfold from the simplest melodic step prevents the listener from focussing on just one such musical pattern. The rising melodic sequence of G#-A leading to A-B, as outlined by the piano in bars 1 and 2, is disrupted by the rhythmic and melodic hesitations of the vocal line (see Example 3.4).

In Beethoven's setting, Goethe's suggestion of a hiccough, or a gulp that marks the effort to expel a single tear, is precisely mirrored in the vocal hiatus after the 'ck' of 'Trocknet' and the following gulping appoggiatura on 'nicht'. The fall of the appoggiatura resists the overall rising sequence, a fall that is mirrored in the piano's decorative descents in the second half of bars 1 and 2. Though the G#-A-B sequence is carried through melodically with a rise to E in bar 3, followed by a balancing descent that marks the four-bar phrase, it is accompanied by continuing internal references to B and A, the pitches of the appoggiatura of bar 1. Beethoven offers this particular oscillation of pitches, like the sounding tear in Goethe's poem, as standing for a moment when time seems halted

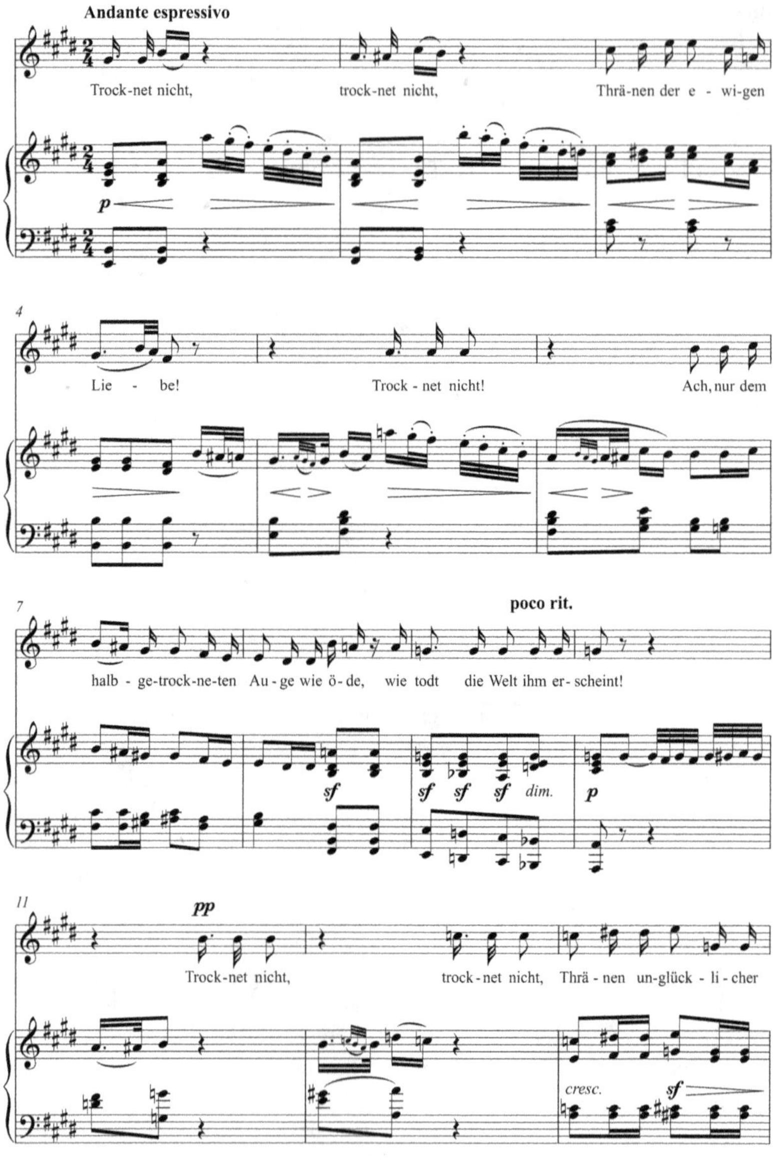

Example 3.4 Beethoven *Wonne der Wehmut*

Example 3.4 (Continued)

by internal resonances of sound. The piano's echo of the voice's original appoggiatura in bar 5 suggests just such a circling back, while the voice comes almost literally to a halt on the single pitch of A. The sequence from the second half of bar 6, whilst expanding the song's tonal canvas, is still presented as circling around the pitches B and A, now projected in tonal as well as harmonic and melodic terms. The song's three marked passages of repetition, at bars 5, 11 and 16, can be heard cumulatively as leading to the climax of bars 19 and 20. But they can also be heard as part of the song's circling impulse, each statement beginning from and moving back to the B–A oscillation. Heard in this way, the final 'Trocknet nicht' of bar 22 acts not so much as an afterthought as a confirmation of the circularity of the whole, with the B-A oscillation finally coming to rest on A-G#, the point from which it first arose. As in Goethe's poem, the tears may expand towards a flow, but the focus in summary is the dropping of a single tear.

In many senses this song is presented as a 'Gesang'; the tonal openness of the first ten-bar statement, with its emphasis on A leading from the repeat in the tonic E of bar 5 to a pause on the dominant of D major in bar 10, suggests a sonata-like impulse. The motivic return of bar 11, which begins from G major, could be termed a 'false' recapitulation, preparing for the 'true' recapitulation in E of bar 16. The keyboard appears to take the lead in making these points of recapitulation, as it gives rhythmic and harmonic impetus to each sequential step. And yet the heart of this sequence, the B-A oscillation, is associated with a detail of vocal articulation, the falling sigh of bar 1. As the keyboard marks the moment of recapitulation in bar 5, it evokes the voice's original catch of breath before the sigh by adding a decorative turn on the dotted rhythm of the first quaver beat. It is as though the keyboardist is seeking to make a precise mimesis of singing in all its physicality. In bar 5, and again in the false recapitulation of bars 11 and 12, the keyboardist is shown to sing and the singer to listen in a provocative exchange of roles. It is as though the keyboardist takes the initiative in bringing the immediacy of vocal production to permeate every aspect of the song, so that enunciation on the breath takes on an almost motivic significance. This is confirmed by the manner of the song's ending. In the final 'Trocknet nicht', the pause in the breath between the syllables of 'Trock' and 'net' is extended even longer, but here the implied articulation is not a catch in the breath but a steady of expulsion of air. The silence after A is now sung through with a descent to the tonic, so that the breath is finally released.

Although *Wonne der Wehmut* belongs in the instrumentally derived tradition of the Viennese keyboard song, Beethoven follows Goethe in seeking to explore the insides of vocality as a radical way of emphasising the intimacy of the lyric. As in Goethe's poem the metaphor of tears takes on a physical substance in sound, so preparing for a performance reality to shape the finished object. The form of the song is in itself highly innovative, drawing the developmental into the circular in a way that prefigures the composer's late style. But in *Wonne der Wehmut* the play with the breath and modes of breathing turns what might have been an abstract proposition into an advocacy for the immediacy of lyric singing – singing in the moment – even in the context of a highly fashioned formal argument. Indeed one might say the formal argument becomes the agency of 'songness', a means of retelling the power of lyric song to convey intimate experience. This exploration of aspects of vocality is also highly significant for Beethoven in forging the radical expressivity of some of his works from the late period. Joseph Kerman points to the role of lyricism and the evocation of voice in the late string quartets as crucial to the composer's play with musical extremes (Kerman, 1966, 195–196). As Richard Kramer points out, there are even hints in the Op. 130 String Quartet in B♭ that the composer was referencing different specific styles of vocal production as a means of indicating how a listener might approach his sprawling multi-movement work (Kramer, 1992, 169). The most obvious contrast is between the steadily sung strophes of the *Cavatina*, the fifth movement, and the gasping recitative that introduces the original finale. An opposition between steady singing and declaiming features in the stop-start impulses of the quartet's first movement. The question-and-answer phrasing either breaks into heavily breathed fragments (as at bar 4 of the opening *Adagio ma non troppo*), or else seeks to establish a continuing flow (as in the *Allegro* that follows from bar 15). It is not just that different kinds of vocality are constantly made to rub shoulders with each other; it is that the listener often cannot be sure which is which. Taken in themselves the first four bars of the first movement could be heard as heightened recitative or as settled song statement. It depends on how one hears or performs the rest in bar 2. The rest can be performed as a measured intake of breath, so encouraging the sense of joining in with the 'answer' of the second two-bar phrase. But the rest can also be performed as a moment of pausing, as though one were pondering where to go next:

Example 3.5 Beethoven Op. 130 String Quartet, first movement, bars 1–7

In Example 3.5 the rest can be heard as inclining the ear backwards, to prepare for the element of repetition as the second two-bar phrase echoes the beginning of the first, or it can be heard to project the ear forwards to the longer rest of bar 4 and the intrusion of a new narrative thought from that point. The difference is registered in a split second of articulation that could clearly go either way; listeners are invited to join the instrumentalists in finding meaning in how they breathe, not as a prefixed decision but in the moment itself. The clarity of the distinction between steady singing and declaiming set out in Op. 130 as a whole allows such instants to emerge as fields of action – as if in such a moment a word were being projected with all its layers of meaning, both explicit and implicit.

With the title of Op. 130's fourth movement, *Alla danza tedesca*, some have thought that Beethoven was referring to the specific singing style of Italian madrigalists mimicking the heaviness of the German language. The idea of instrumentalists pretending to be singers is mirrored here in the notion of Italians pretending to be Germans. Details of swell and shape that should be incidental to the flow of phrasing become unexpectedly prominent, as one can see from the lurching dynamic gradations of the first eight bars of the movement and the rests inserted against the grain into the first and third bars of the first violin's four-bar phrases:

Example 3.6 Beethoven Op. 130 String Quartet, fourth movement, bars 1–8 (first violin)

If one were literally to follow Beethoven's markings then a hiccough or gulp would isolate the repeated Gs of bars 2, 4, 6 and 8 – including the F#s that lead away and then back to G – as the main sounding point of this supposed melody. As in *Wonne der Wehmut*, Beethoven's articulation pulls the ear's attention towards a single obsessive focus to counteract the usual progress of time. The melody of Example 3.6 undergoes an extensive process of variation, with spiralling textures that stretch each instrument's capabilities. However, at its denouement the movement's textures disintegrate into a single line of one-bar fragments passed between the instruments (see Example 3.7).

Example 3.7 Beethoven Op. 130 String Quartet, fourth movement, bars 129–136

Significantly, this statement begins with the isolated focus on G implied by Example 3.6. The backwards then forwards rendering of the melody enacts the standing still in time implied by the original articulation. The instrumentalists are forced to present musical gobbledegook, unless one hears the exhalation of G as complete in itself, as each successive one-bar fragment echoes G or leans towards it. For that one needs to treat each fragment as though it were a word or syllable completed on the breath, conceived as a unit of meaning that belongs both within and outside the immediate context. With poetry one takes such layers for granted, as the performed musicality of words counterpoints with their meaning in the narrated sequence. Meaning happens instantly in the moment, meaning happens over time, and the enunciation of the word or syllable brings those two dimensions into play. A musical motif might seem to offer a similar double focus, but without a sense of the enunciation of the breath it can lose some of the immediacy of engaging with the experience of time itself – the details of time held or time passing. At this point of denouement Beethoven confirms not just the circular impulse of the whole, the focus back on a single moment, but that the instrumentalists must find a way for this moment to be understood as sung.

This is just one instance of the references to song and singing in the late quartets, of the instruments presuming to retell the message of songs such as *Wonne der Wehmut* by means of their enhanced formal and textural dimensions. A work such as Op. 130 certainly succeeds in opening up far greater questions about the mysteries of time than any individual lyric song. Indeed, the very scope of those questions creates a sense of incommensurability which does not sit easily with the nature of the lyric. As has already been noted, though Goethe believes that the lyric is often 'unreasonable' in relation to its details, he says it should be 'reasonable' as a whole (Goethe, 1998, 16). The existence of two possible finales to Op. 130, whatever the circumstances of their composition, confirms that the work's contrasting centripetal-centrifugal impulses could be extended into a notional infinity. The lyric may open doors to eternity; Goethe clearly had the lyric in mind when he encouraged Eckermann to 'hold fast to the present'. But the idea of holding fast to the present suggests the listener should be able to identify a single point of time when developmental play resolves into simplicity.

It is doubtful whether one would pursue links between the late quartets and lyricism with such intensity, were it not for the Ninth Symphony's explicit engagement with song. Although much of the finale to the Ninth is based on showing off instrumental resources, it is song models that are shown to emerge triumphant, as the listener is taken through a series of tests of what it means to sing. The famous instrumental recitatives that follow the finale's opening 'cry of terror' mimics vocal delivery in the most explicit way possible. It also highlights the aesthetic challenge of the lyric, which is to find a way of taking personal enunciation as a basis for communal expression. The practical conundrum of who leads this recitative – whether the conductor, the leader of the cellos or the double basses – mirrors the internal question of how the impulses that give rise to meaning come to be shared. Beethoven does not necessarily help the practical challenge with his instruction 'in the manner of a recitative, but in tempo'. It is noticeable that there are no notated rests during the first of his recitatives; the three-crotchet worth of rests that precede the sequence is implied as a sufficient intake of breath to last the whole sequence. But in his second recitative the insertion of a rest before the final five-note fragment implies the backwards-forwards hesitation that marks a potential change in the experience of time, even if following a steady metronome mark. These five notes can be heard as echoing the cadential fall of the previous bar, or as anticipating the contracted two-note figures that come with the subsequent reprise of the Ninth's first movement. Beethoven mimics not just the breathing of vocal production, but the moment of a memory being triggered as so characteristic of the lyric impulse. Without such a sense of the recitative being sung, the finale's boxes of recapitulation can seem strangely mechanistic, as though the composer were merely advertising his finale as a triumphant answer to the question 'what next'. Yet if the listener is able to engage with the intimacy of the instruments' breathing, to experience the possibilities of space within the progress of time, then each return can be heard as part of a layering of past and present, or even as time standing still. The insertion of the 'Ode to Joy' theme as the fourth of the cameos introduced by the instrumental recitative is often seen as confirmation of the recitative's narrative function; from bar 92 (*Allegro assai*) the cellos and basses are given the role of ushering in the material that will fill the rest of the movement. However, it is noticeable that the immediate trigger for the 'Ode to Joy' theme is not the recitative so much as fragments from the Ninth's third movement uttered by the wind in bars 75–76. Thus the 'Ode to Joy' melody is also presented as arising from a lyric-like moment of lingering to hear echoes from the past.

In some senses the 'Ode to Joy' tune literally comes out of the past, being closely based on the melody of Beethoven's earlier setting of Bürger's *Gegenliebe*. Yet this sense of working from and with memory is not simply left to the appreciation of Beethoven song enthusiasts. The composer recasts his original melody to weave more references to the song's first four-bar phrase into the 24-bar pattern of the strophe. In *Gegenliebe* the strophe follows an *A-B-A* shape, with *B* based on *A* but distinct from it (see FIGURE 3.1). In the 'Ode to Joy' melody the *B* section is infiltrated with *A* as its second four-bar phrase returns to the shape of the opening (see *x2* in FIGURE 3.2).

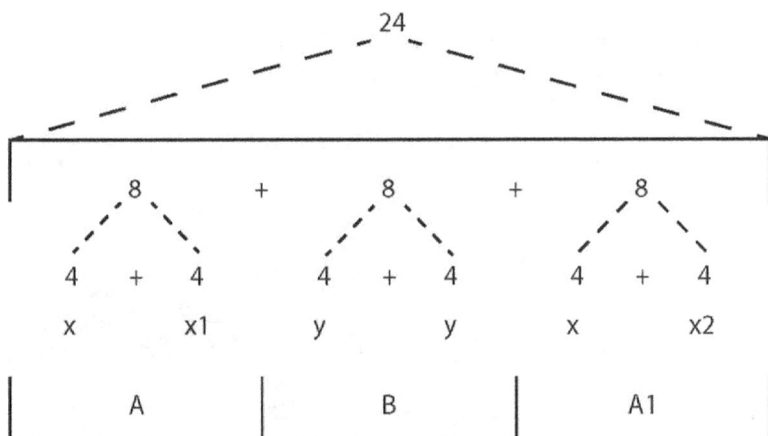

Figure 3.1 Gegenliebe phrasing

This extra degree of internal repetition means that the listener hears the melody as swirling round on one spot, *A* merging into *B* in a playful presentation of the blurring effects of memory. The orientation of the

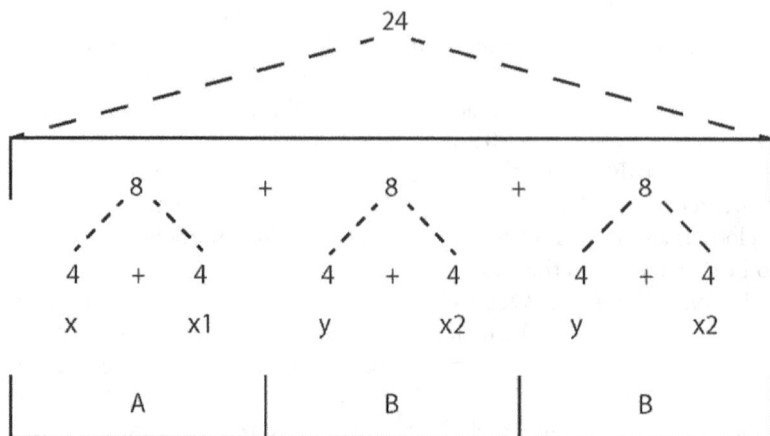

Figure 3.2 'Ode to Joy' phrasing

melody's progression through time is compromised by the lack of distinction between *A* and *B*, and the uncertainty about what marks the point
of strophic return at the 24-bar point – since the opening phrase *x* has
returned so much already. If one compares even the first eight bars of the
'Ode to Joy' melody (Example 3.8) with the first bars of *Gegenliebe*
(Example 2.4), one notices the greater degree of internal repetition.

Example 3.8 Beethoven Ninth Symphony, fourth movement, bars 140–163 (first
violin)

The repetition draws the ear from a four-bar to a two-bar phrase,
and then to a single bar as the basic unit of attention. Indeed it is at the

one-bar level that one begins to find the clearest distinctions of shape. The dotted rhythm of the fourth bar in Example 3.8 begins to assert itself as something different, so anticipating the effect of the contrasting one-bar shapes of *y* within the melody's *B* section.

As typical of the late style, Beethoven embarks on a process of melodic atomisation, even as he also draws the ear to note bigger and bigger circles with the generative energy of his *A-B-B* structures. Centripetal and centrifugal forces vie for supremacy within melodic shapes that – particularly with stringed instruments dominating the first three statements of the 'Ode to Joy' melody (bars 92–164) – can circle without seeming to pause for breath. The representation of the circularity of song seems to transcend actual song boundaries and their association with the physicality of singing. However, when a more obvious symphonic momentum begins to take off after the fourth repeat of the 'Ode to Joy' melody, the fabric collapses into an unexpectedly urgent song-like phrase:

Example 3.9 Beethoven Ninth Symphony, fourth movement, bars 203–206 (first violin)

These halting repetitions, with their divergent harmonic articulation, suggest three voices pulling in different directions before the unanimity of bar 206. More explicitly, they invoke the breathing out of words, so anticipating the vocality of the returning 'cry of terror' two bars later, with its evocation of many shouting voices being called to order by the solo baritone. The 'Freunde' addressed in the baritone's recitative must surely include the mass of instrumentalists who have just been heard, as well as the chorus of singers to come. And the call 'to be more pleasing' might not only apply to the immediate sound of fractured voices, but also to the preceding presentation of the 'Ode to Joy' tune. If so, then the baritone soloist confirms the message that the previous exposition of melody is not in itself sufficient to make the instruments be heard as song. It is not just that the adding of poetic words, with their reference to joy making the singers drunk with fire, gives greater significance to the infectious circularity of the melodic phrases. It is also that the presence of voices superimposes a clear call and response pattern onto the potentially confusing circles of *A-B-B*:

Call Response
A–B B

The second *B* is separated out as a refrain by the interjection from the chorus at the same point in each of the three verses. There is also a four-bar tag inserted before the soloists pick up the next verse, to indicate how the voices take breath before the new 'call'. The invitation to join in, expressed by Schiller's poem, can thus be heard through the disposition of the voices, particularly when compared to the instruments' more neutral version. The previous confusion for listeners, over whether to concentrate on the motivic variation at the level of the eight-, four-, two- or one-bar unit, is here resolved by the clear grammatical hierarchy of Schiller's words (that of syllable, word, phrase and sentence) and by the hierarchy of the vocal breath. The solo singers might be invited to overlap phrases as in the melismatic flourishes of the third vocal strophe (from bar 60 of the vocal *Allegro assai*), but the chorus continues to hammer out basic four-bar breath shapes in simpler versions of the soloists' material. Schiller's text, which presumes to reach to the heavens, is delivered through the steady accumulation of four-bar phrases, as summed up in the chorus's climactic statement 'Und der Cherub steht vor Gott' from bar 85.

The sense of unanimity – many voices singing as one voice – at this point is challenged harmonically by a dramatic sidestep, from the dominant A major to F major as the dominant of B♭. The harmonic conjunction of A and B♭ recalls the dissonant fragmentation of the 'cry of terror'. Texturally such fragmentation is taken even further by the isolated groans issuing from the bassoon, contrabassoon and bass drum in the following *Alla Marcia*. Yet rhythmically, four-bar breath shapes emerge triumphant even from such extreme disintegration. Groans soon turn into the clearest possible punctuation for the returning song shapes of the 'Ode of Joy'. When the punctuation of the trumpet is added to the shapes of the bassoon/contrabassoon, there can be no doubt about the hierarchy of the phrasing of 'Ode to Joy'. Patterns of call and response are now rendered with the precision of an army moving in step around the squares of a parade ground. The change to march-like articulation is clearly evident in the solo tenor's rendering of Schiller's text; the addition of rests to his line suggests a gasping of the breath to keep up with the momentum of the feet. Yet if each two bars of this new *Alla Marcia* section are taken as the equivalent of one bar of the previous exposition of the 'Ode to Joy', then solo tenor and answering chorus keep to the 24-bar shape, with a four-bar turn around, of the original strophes. It seems that the strophic patterns of lyric song are able to incorporate processes of variation. One might even say that singing in time to the tread of feet adds a sense of invincibility to the breathing of song's steady periodic phrases.

The song-like steadiness is challenged once the rhythmic pace changes from walking to running; the voices drop out at the onrush of instrumentally driven compound quavers from bar 101 of the *Alla Marcia*. The fugue-like subject which accompanies this change begins with a four-bar shape taken from the 'Ode to Joy' tune, but the entries soon splinter into two- and then one-bar patterns of repetition. The immediacy of song disappears, but the length of this instrumental fugato episode still bears relationship to the larger strophic measurements that accompany the 'Ode to Joy'. It covers a span of 112 bars, roughly the equivalent of two strophes, with the point between the 'verses' being marked in bar 491 by the tonal shift from B♭ to B. The clear markers of the tenor's strophe before and the definite return to the 'Ode to Joy' afterwards (in bar 213) frame the fugato as part of a four-verse presentation of the 'Ode to Joy' in compound duple metre, matching the original four-verse exposition of the 'Ode to Joy' as set out by the instruments at the beginning of the finale. Thus a kind of pattern of meta-strophes begins to emerge across the movement with each new version of the 'Ode to Joy' being set off by emphatic silences, as though exaggerating the pause for taking breath that happens with strophes at the immediate level. The first meta-strophe of the 'Ode to Joy' – the instrumental exposition of the first *Allegro assai* – emerges from the silences of the preceding instrumental recitative, whilst the second – the vocal exposition of the second *Allegro assai* – emerges from the silences surrounding the entry of the solo baritone. These silences are less obvious perhaps than the pause out of which the bassoon and contrabassoon make their noises at the start of the *Alla Marcia*. It is as if an extra large intake of breath is necessary if this change of tonality, metre, tempo, key and character is to be absorbed into the song continuity. The abrupt halt in bar 264 of the *Alla Marcia*, cutting short the four-bar turnaround at the end of the previous 'Ode to Joy' statement, is more dramatic still. This manner of introducing the *Andante maestoso* prepares the section as the greatest interruption yet to the flow of song repetitions. The blurring of the downbeat, and even the uncertain sense of pulse, as the chorus declaims 'Seid umschlungen Millionen', echoes the recitative style of the finale's opening rather than the periodic phrasing of the 'Ode to Joy', a connection that is underlined by the prominence of the cellos and basses in leading the voices.

One could even say that here the finale is referencing the angular profile of many of the melodic lines of the Ninth's first movement (see Example 3.10). Although, in the above example, the tutti orchestra clearly marks the two- and four-bar phrasing by joining the bassoon's punctuation, these sequences follow an additive principle; each phrase pushes forwards rather than circling back in patterns of question and answer, call and response.

Example 3.10 Beethoven Ninth Symphony, first movement, bars 138–142 (woodwind)

That is why in his essay 'On Performing Beethoven's Ninth Symphony' Wagner highlighted this phrase as so hard for the orchestra to sing, to the extent that he felt a bit of editing was needed to make each phrase more amenable to a sense of flow (Jacobs, 1979, 112–118). Similarly, in the *Andante maestoso*, although the statements of bars 1–8 and bars 17–24 follow each other in repeated eight-bar blocks, the harmonic modulation between them disrupts an immediate sense of question-and-answer phrasing. Beethoven is writing out a kind of choral recitative, where the voices have to feel their way into unanimity through the continuing rhythmic punctuation of four-bar phrases. In Schiller's poem the entry of the 'Seid umschlungen' marks a shift in the rhyming patterns to emphasise how a communal voice – this is the first chorus within Schiller's original ode – can swiftly accommodate itself to sing as one. Beethoven also gives emphasis at this point to the basic rhythmic functions of song, as blocks of phrasing continue even without the surface ingredients of periodic melody. In setting the next chorus from Schiller's poem – 'Ihr stürzt neider' – Beethoven dissolves the sense of melody even further. In bars 42 to 49 the soprano line is reduced to a bare scalic ascent from B♭ to G. As this climactic G is picked up by the instrumental mass from bar 53, as the highest pitch of a shimmering dominant minor ninth on A, the notion of individual voice seems to disappear. However, the marking of four- and eight-bar phrasing is still prominent, even at this point of textural dissolution. Although the dominant minor ninth refers to the superimposition of A and B♭ that marked the opening of the finale, there is no actual return to the rhythmic confusion that marked the 'cry of terror'. Rather, the steadiness of song breaths holds throughout the *Adagio ma non troppo*. The instrumental prelude at the head of the section establishes the measure of the four-bar unit, as in a traditional song introduction. Once this instrumental unit is repeated by the voices to create an arch of four-plus-four bars, it projects a sense of shape for the eight bars to come. There is no clear vocal cadence to mark the end of 16 bars, but the exaggerated silence at the beginning of bar 49 marks an obvious intake of breath as at a strophe's midway point. Though this is followed by a climactic four-bar statement of 'Über Sternen muß er wohnen' in bars 49–52, another silence at the beginning of bar 53 suggests a further intake of breath. With the subsequent textural stasis it is as though the breath is held suspended for four, eight, twelve bars, until the huge release that comes with the return of the 'Ode to Joy' tune at the *Allegro energico*. The return of the 'Ode to Joy' melody is bound in as an answer to the phrasing of the previous section, as the point where the breath is exhaled to its fullest extent.

Heard in this way, through the rhythms of vocal breathing, the sections of the *Andante maestoso*, the *Adagio ma non troppo* and the *Allegro energico* can be understood as part of another meta strophe. They become drawn into an experience of song, the linking of strophe to the expansion and contraction of the breath, even if on the surface they draw in styles that might seem more symphonic in origin. Such a process of song absorbing symphony is confirmed by the disjunct lines of the 'Seid umschlungen' being combined with the 'Ode to Joy' melody at the beginning of the *Allegro energico*. Yet there is still the possibility that the symphonic might be understood as emerging predominant. Much of the section which follows the arrival of the *Allegro energico* is made up of free repetitions of musical and poetic material, as in an operatic finale. However, there is one passage that explicitly recalls the power of song when linked to the intimacy of breathing. The recapitulation of Schiller's chorus 'Ihr stürzt nieder' (bars 76 to 91 of the *Allegro energico*) is marked by a return to the extreme fragmentation of the opening of the symphony, where each two-note figure appeared in danger of falling into a vacuum of rests. Except that the syllabic articulation of the current passage, with each syllable being enunciated on the breath, suggests the void filling as a syllable connects to a word and a word to a phrase. After 16 bars of such exertion, the sense of the breath is able to transfer from the intervallic fragments to the overarching span. The potential fracturing as of a single voice is shown transforming into communal expression, culminating in the chorale-like statement at bar 91 of 'Brüder über Sternenzelt Muß ein lieber Vater wohnen'. The resulting 34-bar statement from bar 76 to

108, before the acceleration of the ensuing *Allegro ma non tanto*, recalls something of the 32-bar strophe of the first 'Seid umschlungen Millionen' (*Andante maestoso*) or the solemn 28 bars of the first 'Ihr stürzt nieder' (*Adagio ma non troppo*). The current passage is not a recapitulation or return in the symphonic manner, more a sense of time standing still as strophes of song are recalled from being held intact in the memory. For all its sprawling dimensions, the connectedness of these strophic shapes in the Ninth's finale ensures that it continues to communicate as song in physical as well as aesthetic ways. In his essay 'On Conducting', Wagner affirmed that the secret of performing the Ninth Symphony lay in the conductor encouraging the instruments to sing at all points (Jacobs, 1979, 55–57). There is certainly much in all the movements that suggests a process of growing melodicisation, of learning how to sing. But in the finale Beethoven appears to embrace not just an advocacy of singing but of song, in the sense of seeking to convey once more the power of song strophes to transcend the passage of time and lay hold of the memory in unexpected and exciting ways.

References

Adorno, Theodor W. *Beethoven: The Philosophy of Music*, ed. Rolf Tiedemann, tr. Edmind Jephcott. Cambridge: Polity Press, 1998.

Baker, Nancy Kovaleff and Christensen, Thomas (eds.). *Aesthetics and Art of Musical Composition in the German Enlightenment: Selected Writings of J.G. Sulzer and H.C. Koch*. Cambridge: Cambridge University Press, 1995.

Boettcher, Hans. *Beethoven als Liederkomponist*. Augsburg, Germany: Sändig, 1974.

Cooper, Barry. *Beethoven*. Oxford: Clarendon Press, 2000.

Dahlhaus, Carl. *Ludwig van Beethoven*, tr. Mary Whittall. Oxford: Clarendon Press, 1991.

Fairley, Barker. *Goethe as Revealed in His Poetry*. New York: Frederick Unger, 1963.

Goethe, Johann Wolfgang von. *Werke*. Volume 1. Stuttgart and Tübingen, Germany: J.G. Cottaschen Buchhandlung, 1827.

Goethe, Johann Wolfgang von. *Werke*. Volume 1, 41. Weimar, Germany: Hermann Böhlau, 1887–1912.

Goethe, Johann Wolfgang von. *Conversations and Encounters*, ed. and tr. David Luke and Robert Pick. London: Oswald Wolff, 1966.

Goethe, Wolfgang von. *Faust*, ed. and tr. Stuart Atkins. Princeton, NJ: Princeton University Press, 1984.

Gray, Ronald. *Goethe: A Critical Introduction*. Cambridge: Cambridge University Press, 1967.

Hamburger, Michael (ed.). *Beethoven: Letters, Journals and Conversations*. London: Thames and Hudson, 1951.

Herzfeld, Marianne von (ed.). *Letters from Goethe*, tr. Marianne von Herzfeld and C. Melvil Sym. Edinburgh: Edinburgh University Press, 1957.

Hölty, Ludwig Christoph Heinrich. *Gedichte*, ed. Friederich Leopold von Stolberg and Johann Heinrich Voss. Hamburg, Germany: Carl, Ernst Bohn, 1783.

Jacobs, Robert L. (tr.). *Three Wagner Essays*. London: Ernst Eulenberg, 1979.

Kerman, Joseph. *The Beethoven Quartets*. New York: W.W. Norton, 1966.

Kinderman, William. *Beethoven*. Oxford: Clarendon Press, 1995.

Kramer, Richard. Between Cavatina and Ouverture: Opus 130 and the Voices of Narrative. *Beethoven Forum* 1, 1992.

Lukács, Georg. *The Theory of the Novel*, tr. Anna Bostock. London: Merlin Press, 1971.

Matthisson, Friederich. *Gedichte*. Volume 1, ed. Gottfried Bölsing. Tübingen, Germany: Litterarische Verein in Stuttgart, 1912.

Reid, Paul. *The Beethoven Song Companion*. Manchester: Manchester University Press, 2007.

Schiller, Friedrich. *On the Aesthetic Education of Man*, ed. and tr. Elizabeth M. Wilkinson and L.A. Willoughby. Oxford: Clarendon Press, 1967.

Schiller, Friedrich. *Sämtliche Werke*. Volume 5, ed. Jost Perfahl. Munich, Germany: Winkler Verlag, 1968.

Staiger, Emil. *Basic Concepts of Poetics*, ed. Marianne Burkhard and Luanne T. Frank, tr. Janette C. Hudson and Luanne T. Frank. University Park, PA: Pennsylvania State University Press, 1991.

Sternfeld, Frederick. *Goethe and Music: A List of Parodies*. New York: New York Public Library, 1954.

Szondi, Peter. *On Textual Understanding and Other Essays*, tr. Harvey Mendelsohn. Minneapolis: University of Minnesota Press, 1986.

4 Lyric legacy

Finding a place for Beethoven song

Writing in 1861 the critic Eduard Hanslick talks of Beethoven's Ninth Symphony causing 'shock and surprise' (Hanslick, 1963, 77). Thirty or so years after the composer's death, he believes the Ninth demands 'devoted and extensive study' (Hanslick, 1963, 72–73), if awe is to be replaced by 'understanding, admiration, and love' (77). Even Wagner, one of the work's biggest devotees, sometimes doubted the Ninth's comprehensibility (Wagner, 1983, 57); he was reassured by Habeneck's performance in 1839 which showed the orchestra finding a way to sing (Jacobs, 1979, 55). Wagner saw this aspect of vocality as crucial to Beethoven's intentions. In his essay 'A Pilgrimage to Beethoven' of 1840, he put these words into Beethoven's mouth:

> Imagine the instruments that convey the primal feelings – those raw wild feelings encompassing the infinite – united with the voice that represents the limited, but clear, definite sensibility of the human heart. That second element, the voice, would have a beneficial effect upon the instruments' expression of the struggle of primal feeling in that it would set it within the framework of a definite, unifying course.
>
> (Wagner, 1994, 80–81)

'Imagine' is perhaps the key word here, for Wagner implies Beethoven is not entirely successful in his searches in the Ninth. 'Definite, unifying course' suggests the symphony resolving into song, not just singing, but Wagner has Beethoven say that the words of Schiller's ode act only as a filler; they cannot be the focus for the finale because even this 'very noble and uplifting poem . . . [is] a very long way from expressing what in this case no poem in the world could possibly utter' (Wagner, 1994, 81). Instead of seeing Beethoven's play with strophe and phrase and breath as a direct means of engaging with Schiller's ode, Wagner suggests such processes should be approached more abstractly, as though the composer were responding to a text that cannot be known or communicated.

It seems clear that what is being adumbrated in 'A Pilgrimage to Beethoven' is Wagner's own struggle with the status of words in his music dramas. He uses Beethoven's Ninth Symphony to articulate his concept of the 'poetic intent', something which both music and words point to as a kind of shadowy presence between them (Glass, 1983). Such shiftiness is very far from the lyric impulse, where the presence of words – in all their sonic and semantic individuality – offers to fill and animate the immediate musical canvas. Despite Wagner's doubts about the worthiness of Schiller's poem, such an impulse can be traced throughout the Ninth's finale. Despite the movement's magnified choral and orchestral dimensions, the listener can still focus on the precise timing of the arrival of the words 'Über Sternen muß er wohnen' as the pivot on which the finale turns. These words – with their suggestion of a circle of stars that can be traced even as they edge into infinity – can be taken as the motivation for the finale's structure, in its details and its whole, in the manner of song. The circle of strophes is linked in specific ways to the imagery of the poem. Yet Wagner implies such a view is too limiting. He may have been thinking of Beethoven's claim that in setting words he always wished to rise above the poet (Hamburger, 1951, 223), or even his apparent dislike of song-writing (186). In an earlier passage from 'A Pilgrimage to Beethoven' Wagner makes the composer refer to *Adelaide* as a mere trifle, one of the things that 'your professional singer takes up because they enable him to display his virtuosity' (Wagner, 1994, 80). Yet if the Ninth is distanced from the parameters of song, then the finale is in danger of falling into a generic vacuum. In *Opera and Drama* Wagner says Beethoven is like Columbus, setting out to find India and instead discovering a new world (Wagner, 1995, 70–71). That new world is the one that Wagner then identifies with his own music drama, with all the trappings that come from needing to define a new genre for listeners. In the meantime Beethoven's Ninth is seen as left hanging. Hanslick too suggests that the Ninth sits on the edge of the unknown; he likens it and the *Missa Solemnis* to the Pillars of Hercules that declare "No farther!' – the one to sacred music, the other to the symphony' (Hanslick, 1963, 73). The Pillars of Hercules are traditionally identified with the Rock of Gibraltar and the Jebel Musa in Morocco, two mountains at the mouth of the Mediterranean which in ancient times were taken as marking the edge of the known world. Such a metaphor, like Wagner's reference to Columbus, implies Beethoven cannot be trusted to leave a legacy without careful handling or reinterpretation. Yet lyric song, by definition, appeals directly to its listeners, calling them to join in without hesitation. If Beethoven's finale is approached by listeners as actual song, then far from leaving them stranded in uncertainty it should draw them towards the familiar. The meta-strophes of the Ninth's finale, outlined in Chapter 3, offer the opportunity for call and response shapes to embrace every aspect of the movement. The question then is whether associating the Ninth with the generic markers of song, so that it is treated as a song symphony rather than simply a choral symphony, diminishes or enhances one's sense of the Ninth's significance. This depends not simply on how one hears the details of the Ninth's finale, as explored in the previous chapter, but on how one views the legacy of Beethoven's involvement with song as a whole. Is there a continuity and also a contiguity of song surrounding the Ninth Symphony to make the designation 'song symphony' appropriate?

If one calls the Ninth a song symphony, then one inevitably invites comparison of Beethoven with Mahler, for whom song was the alpha and omega of his composing life. Many commentators have outlined how the Wunderhorn songs provide material and inspiration for Mahler's symphonies (Mitchell, 1975; Johnson, 2009). This song association is taken as highly significant for Mahler, yet there are also ways in which it can be connected to the pervasive influence of Beethoven's Ninth. In his First Symphony Mahler highlights the issue of the compositional weight accorded to the finale. In the Second Symphony this is added to by a choral dimension, indeed the introduction of Klopstock's words brings Mahler perilously close to shadowing Beethoven's recourse to Schiller's ode in the Ninth. In the Third Symphony the composer's exploration of symphonic endings continues with an unexpected twist. Words are now removed from the finale, but repetitions of a song tune take centre stage in a way reminiscent of the first instrumental presentation of the 'Ode to Joy' in Beethoven's Ninth Symphony. Mahler's Fourth Symphony can then be heard to complete the sequence with a song setting which explicitly draws on the composer's Wunderhorn heritage, just as Beethoven drew on the Göttinger Hainbund associations of Bürger's *Gegenliebe* in setting Schiller's ode.

The ending of Mahler's Fourth Symphony, 'Das himmlische Leben', belongs in a song anthology in the way Beethoven's Ninth finale does not. It is true that the 24 bars of the 'Ode to Joy' strophe are regularly used as an anthem or hymn tune, but one could not arrange the whole of the finale for voice and piano in the pattern of 'Das himmlische Leben'. Mahler's implied pairing of 'Das himmlische Leben' with the Wunderhorn song 'Das irdische Leben' underlines this dual generic identity. The instrumental ritornello that interrupts the calm at the close of the first verse of 'Das himmlische Leben' is linked to both the opening of the first movement of the Fourth Symphony and a quotation from the prelude to 'Das irdische Leben'. The alternation of major and minor mode strophes is linked to both the double variation structure of the Fourth's third movement and the alternation between the anguished calls of the child and the more reassuring tones of the mother in 'Das irdische Leben'. In 'Das himmlische Leben' Mahler confirms that song and symphony can co-reside, as he expands and collapses our sense of aural dimensions through the cycle of strophic repetitions. The clearly marked units of 'Das irdische Leben', with their distinctions between vocal statement and instrumental ritornello, are echoed in the symphonic finale with the juxtaposition of vocal chorale-like refrain with the instrumental sound of the 'fool's bells'. Yet at the opening of 'Das himmlische Leben' Mahler creates an expanded melodic arch that promises to transcend such boundaries. At the close of the movement he makes a dual reference point with the final *morendo* rocking motif. On the one hand it proclaims the punctuation of song – like the closing fourths of *Hans und Grethe*, one of Mahler's earliest songs. But the *morendo* instruction also indicates an edging into infinity, like the shimmering dominant minor ninth sonority of 'Über Sternen muß er wohnen' in the finale of Beethoven's Ninth. The merging with silence can be linked to the most famous of all such gestures, the *pianissimo* fifths at the opening of Beethoven's Ninth. This is often seen as evoking a new sound world for the symphony, a gesture that Bruckner was to copy many times. But Mahler here encourages the listener to hear such a moment with the ears of song.

The end of Mahler's Fourth Symphony is referenced quite specifically in the work that stands in the place of a Ninth Symphony, *Das Lied von der Erde*. From Figure 64 of the final song, 'Der Abschied', the voice's sevenfold repetition of the single word 'ewig' creates a kind of rocking in slow motion, with the resting point on C being finally suspended. The removal of the tonic suggests the openness of symphonic dimensions; the voice's melodic motion at this point has even been linked to the opening of Mahler's next work, the symphony he entitled his Ninth. But Mahler counterpoints the motion of the voice with a more immediate rocking figure of alternating thirds in the harp, a figure which punctuates much of the movement. As in the Fourth's finale this rocking echoes the gestures of song accompaniment even if, in this case, the periodic phrasing of song often seems to be absent. In the final song of *Das Lied von der Erde* strophic structures expand towards the meta-strophe, as with aspects of Beethoven's Ninth, but at the close Mahler suggests the symphonic can still be heard as song, should the listener choose to do so.

Both Mahler's Fourth Symphony and *Das Lied von der Erde* can be taken as encouraging listeners to hear Beethoven's Ninth Symphony with the ears of song, to join in with its strophic shapes of call and response – whether projected on the smallest or the largest scale. One might even say that there is something distinctly Mahlerian in the cross-referral that Beethoven makes between his actual song *Gegenliebe*, his *Choral Fantasy* Op. 80 and the Ninth's finale. The Bürger-derived song material tran- scends its original context and continues to be quoted and extracted, with aspects being reconceived for a new context in a way that could be likened to the relationship between Mahler's *Lieder eines fahrenden Gesellen* and his First Symphony. Beethoven's *Choral Fantasy* of 1808 postdates his setting of Bürger's *Gegenliebe* by almost 15 years. There is a sense of the composer looking back to the melodic essence of the earlier song as the original 24-bar strophe is contracted into 16 bars for the choral setting of 'Schmeichelnd hold', so that the *A-B-A* structure of the strophe in *Gegenliebe* (FIGURE 3.1) is replaced by *A-B* (FIGURE 4.1):

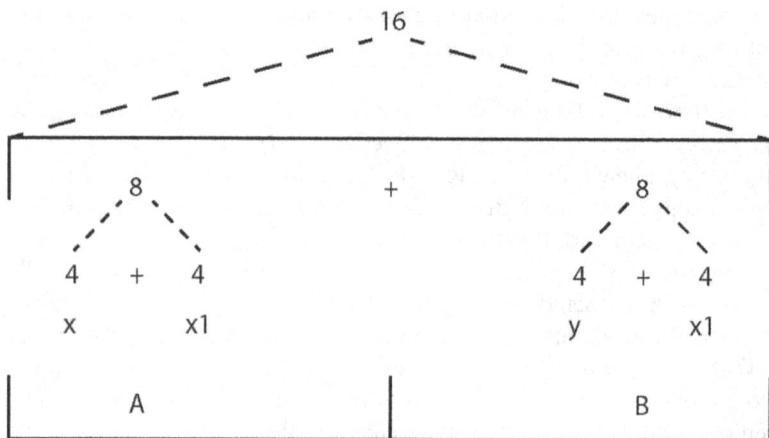

Figure 4.1 Choral Fantasy 'Schmeichelnd hold' phrasing

Some echo of *Gegenliebe*'s dramatic pauses, as the singer waits for the beloved to reply before the reprise of the song's *A* section, is heard in the fermata which precedes the return of *x1* within the *B* section of the *Choral Fantasy*. But otherwise the neatness and symmetry of the phras- ing suggests a certain distancing from the urgency of the original Bürger poem. In the *Choral Fantasy* both the *A* and the *B* sections divide into four-bar question-and-answer units, which unfold in the first instrumen- tal theme and variations section of the *Meno allegro* of the finale with dance-like precision. It is no surprise to hear that when Beethoven commissioned a poem to fill the *Choral Fantasy*'s closing *Allegretto, ma non troppo* choral presentation of the tune, he had the choral parts already written. Beethoven's setting of the words here is actually less clumsy than it is in *Gegenliebe*, where he makes the singer almost fall over the rhythms of Bürger's text. Christoph Kuffner's poem slides in smoothly as though creating minimum disturbance, as befits its subject matter. The newly commissioned text enthuses over the existing harmonies of life ('Lebens Harmonien'), unlike Bürger's *Gegenliebe* which pleads with the beloved for a harmony yet to happen.

In the *Choral Fantasy* it is as though song were being viewed from the wrong end of a telescope. Like the rhapsodic toccata-like sections for solo piano, the song tune – whether with or without words – creates islands of clearly characterised material. The tune is heralded with portentous upbeats in the oboes and horns at the beginning of the *Meno allegro* – upbeats that are reprised before the moment of the choral entry in the closing *Allegretto, ma non troppo* – but once introduced the song material flattens out to make each detail seem less important. The one obvious exception is the setting of the word 'Kraft', which is extracted by a harmonic step to the flat submediant in the closing section of the work. It is as though a shudder passes through the easy 'harmony' – of music and poem, question-and-answer phrasing – as with the sudden side-step from A major to F major at the words 'vor Gott' before the *Alla Marcia* section of the Ninth's finale. In the *Choral Fantasy* such a sidestep comes as an afterthought, to add perspective to cadences that are already closing triumphantly upon the tonic. In the words of Kuffner's poem, God's favour comes where love and strength ('Kraft') are united. The union has already happened, the favour is ensured; this is not a plea to find strength to stand before God. The word 'Kraft' is thrown up as part of the sublime delight ('Hochgefühl') in life's harmoniousness. And yet the word clearly meant something special to Beethoven. After the completion of the *Choral Fantasy* Beethoven wrote to his publisher Breitkopf & Härtel:

> You may wish to print another text, as the text like the music was written very quickly. . . . Still with another set of words I want the word *Kraft* to be kept or one similar to it in its place.
>
> (Beethoven, 1972, 106)

As an example of what song can do, the sounding of this one word becomes a kind of talisman for the composer ensuring meaning. Its harmonic resonance actually comes from within the song tune. The move to the flat submediant echoes the momentary flatwards slip to the subdominant – the B♭ that is added to the tonic C – at the point of returning to *x1* in the *B* section of the melody (see FIGURE 4.1). The rhyming of melodic return is clouded with a sense of 'if only', so presaging the need for 'strength' to hold these chiming phrases together.

Song's attention to detail – the detail of words and music – encourages the incidental to become something significant, even momentous. The 'Kraft' moment in the *Choral Fantasy* indeed operates as a defining element within the Ninth Symphony, and not just in the finale. In the Ninth's first movement a melodic move to the flat submediant B♭ in bar 24, the most sustained instrumental voicing up to this point, is accompanied by an unexpected harmonic sidestep from G minor to E♭ major. This plunge flatwards sets up B♭ as a challenge to the tonic D – in melodic, harmonic and tonal terms – for the rest of the symphony. The opposition between D and B♭ breaks out dramatically at the opening of the finale in the B♭-A dissonance of the 'cry of terror', an opposition which re-echoes in the 'vor Gott' moment mentioned above and in the sonorities of the 'Über Sternen muß er wohnen'. The shimmering textures that accompany this latter phrase specifically recall the textures of the symphony's opening. Yet the formal placing of such a harmonic moment is also highly reminiscent of the *Choral Fantasy* and *Gegenliebe*, since it coincides with the tipping back to the main song tune – the return to the 'Ode to Joy' at the *Allegro energico* – just as with those earlier rounds of song. As with Mahler, the symphony does not just quote song material; lines of connection and progression emerge that encourage the whole symphony to be heard in song-like terms.

The connections between Beethoven's Ninth and his *Choral Fantasy* are clear at many levels; Beethoven himself referred to them (Kinderman, 1995, 132). But it is interesting to note that the composer did not fall into using Schiller's text simply as a substitute for Kuffner's poem, in the way he suggested to Breitkopf & Härtel. The poetic rhythms of the 'Ode to Joy' might just be shoehorned into the *Choral Fantasy's A-B* structures, if one was not too particular about word-setting. As it is, the Ninth's finale recasts the earlier melody to begin on the downbeat rather than the half-bar, so emphasising the syllables of 'Freude' as the energy galvanising the circles of repetition. The repeat of the poetry and music of the *B* section in the 'Ode to Joy' also adds to the excitement of the return to *A*; the calm symmetry of *A-B* song sections in the *Choral Fantasy* is replaced by the urgency to find a way back to the basic eight-bar song-statement of *A* after the call-and-response statement given to *B*. There is a strenuousness connected with each articulation of the strophe that draws on the aspirational nature of Schiller's poem, which seeks to link worm and Cherub, falling down and reaching beyond the stars. The stamping energy of Schiller's word 'Freude' – its sound and meaning – is shown to inspire the creation of something new out of the preexisting song material. If the *Choral Fantasy* suggests a certain distancing from poetry on the composer's part, the Ninth finale suggests him bringing it back near. The Ninth postdates the *Choral Fantasy* by 16 years, slightly longer than the period separating the *Choral Fantasy* from *Gegenliebe*. Yet the trajectory is not so much a further development away from simple song, as a new embracing of what the most immediate elements of song might offer. The shouts of 'Freude', as Schiller's ode is introduced, bind word and music together in a way that contrasts markedly with the 'Schmeichelnd hold' repetitions of the *Choral Fantasy*. Even in the song *Gegenliebe* the isolated repetitions of 'wüßt ich' that prepare for the return of the opening stanza (bars 128 and 130) lack generative energy compared to the explosive power of 'Freude'. In his Schiller setting Beethoven shows how the impetus of 'Freude' passes on down the line, as the stamping inflexion connected with that particular word spills over into the setting of 'schöner', 'funken', and 'Töchter'.

If one did not know the *Gegenliebe* and *Choral Fantasy* models for the 'Ode to Joy' tune, one might believe that 'Freude' had inspired an entirely new melody. But in fact such questions of which comes first, music or word, already suggest a distancing from the lyric impulse where either word or music can be taken as a starting point because each bears the imprint of the other. For Herder, as Matthew Gelbart points out, this basic synergy of words and music shines best from folksong models (Gelbart, 2007, 198). The ideal, according to the Herder-inspired Reichardt, is for composers to find a 'Weise' (tune) in song so that one can no longer think of the melody without the words or the words without the melody (Reichardt, 1782, 3). He suggests such selflessness may rub against the grain for many composers:

> Even for our composers, who imagine they have reached the highest pinnacle, it remains the hardest task to make a song in the true spirit of the folk.
>
> (Reichardt, 1782, 5)

He praises the North German songster Schulz for leading the way, a composer who might seem furthest from Beethoven in every regard. But there are signs that Beethoven, like Schulz and Reichardt, continued to revere Herder's view of song. His setting of Herder's *Der Gesang der Nachtigall* from 1813 has unexpectedly Schulzian qualities, to the extent that it seems more a nursery rhyme than an art song. It has the 'quality of a unison' that Reichardt recognises as the hallmark of folksong

(Reichardt, 1782, 3), the keyboard part being mostly consigned to drones or shadowing the turns of the vocal line with parallel thirds and sixths:

Example 4.1 Beethoven *Der Gesang der Nachtigall*, bars 7–15

The obsessive melodic circling also suggests a 'ring-a-ring-a-roses' character, much like Schulz's setting of Voss's *Im Grünen* (see Example 4.2).

Example 4.2 Schulz *Im Grünen*

Beethoven's tune in Example 4.1 sits down upon the tonic even more than Schulz's. He relies upon the distinctive quality of the refrain to give direction to the whole; without it the song might pass as a blur. There is indeed a provocative aspect to Beethoven's flattening of melodic detail here. The string of revolving thirds and seconds both mimics a night-ingale's song and tests the ear to try to catch the small-scale patterns which emerge from the trills of the prelude. Coming from 1813, this song might even be heard to anticipate the late style's obsessive treat-ment of melody. Yet perhaps the most distinctive aspect of *Der Gesang der Nachtigall* is that it cannot be conceived without words. Even more than with the 'Freude' impulse of the 'Ode to Joy', this song relies upon the kick and impetus of syllabic enunciation; one cannot imagine the melody being rendered instrumentally like the 'Ode to Joy' in the preludial sec-tions of the Ninth's finale. Such a tongue-twister is all about spitting out words and making them bond with the tune, particularly as the verbal mix of dactyls and trochees shifts slightly from stanza to stanza. As Reich-ardt says of a folksong, the melody is all for the words, it does not exist for itself alone.

One might think of this song being intended as a special tribute to Herder, or as an accompanying piece to the folksong arrangements that Beethoven was busy making for George Thomson during this period. There is certainly clear melodic kinship between *Der Gesang der Nachtigall* and such a song as 'Bonny Laddie, Highland Laddie', which Barry Cooper dates from 1814–1815 (Cooper, 1994, 23). The breathless revolving thirds and seconds of the Scottish song mimic the excitement of a highland reel, but again it is the spitting out of the words – in this case 'Bonny Laddie, Highland Laddie' recurs every two bars – that propels the line. It is interesting that Beethoven asked to have the words as well as melodies from Thomson, though without much success (Cooper, 1994, 69–92). It seems he wanted to approach the songs as songs, not simply as interesting melodies for instrumental arrangement. He may even have wished to draw on the specific energy of the vocal inflexions for generating his instrumental responses. One imagines the composer's frustration at looking at Thomson's pages of songs without words. But in a sense this too was a Herderian exercise. When publishing his influential *Volkslieder* Herder offered his readers folksong poems without music, with the implication that with such material if you had one, you had both; the music is quite literally in the words. Taking the case of *Heidenröslein*, perhaps the most famous item in Herder's collections, the words themselves can be traced back to both poetic and musical sources from the sixteenth and earlier seventeenth centuries (Sternfeld, 1954, 120–121). What Herder presents in 1773 as 'Es sah ein Knab ein Rößlein stehn' is not so much a poem as a 'Weise'; the multiple versions of the text offered by both Herder and Goethe are to be understood as continuing echoes from one essential folk-like song. As with 'Bonny Laddie, Highland Laddie' the sense of continuity is heard most clearly in the hammering of the essential trochee, there 'Laddie' here 'Rößlein'.

In the version which Herder published in his *Von Deutscher Art und Kunst* the trochaic impetus of 'Rößlein' is hidden, as with the upbeats of 'Es', 'Ein' and 'Er' in the first verse, until the refrain gets into swing in the last two lines:

> Es sah' ein Knab' ein Rößlein stehn
> Ein Rößlein auf der Heiden.
> Er sah, es war so frisch und schön
> Und bleib stehn, es anzusehen
> Und stand in süssen Freuden:
> Rößlein, Rößlein, Rößlein roth,
> Rößlein auf der Heiden!
> (Herder, 1773, 57)

The version of this poem which Goethe published in 1789 makes the hammered rhythm of 'Röslein' dominate from the first line:

Sah ein Knab ein Röslein stehn,
Röslein auf der Heiden,
Was so jung und morgenschön,
Lief er schnell es nah zu sehn,
Sahs mit vielen Freuden.
Röslein, Röslein, Röslein rot,
Röslein auf der Heiden.
                    (Goethe, 1986, 10)

In their settings Reichardt and Schubert both begin with repeated notes and dancing-on-the-spot rhythms, again to foreground the weight of the refrain. Beethoven too came under the spell of the *Heidenröslein* challenge. His sketches for a setting include one from as late as 1820 where a lilting triple metre masks the trochaic impulse almost entirely (Nottebohm, 1872, 50, 1887, 137, 471, 474, 576). This sketch is close to a version from a much earlier period, 1796; one might interpret it as Beethoven seeking to hold onto the melodic sophistication of a Viennese keyboard song. Yet in between, in 1818, comes a sketch that is much closer to the style of *Der Gesang der Nachtigall*:

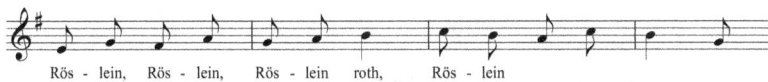

Rös - lein, Rös - lein, Rös - lein roth, Rös - lein

Example 4.3 Beethoven *Heidenröslein* (sketch from 1818)

Crucially this sketch begins with the refrain, the heart of the matter. It is tantalisingly short, with no real clue over whether the song is to be in G major or E minor. But one knows enough to appreciate the vein Beethoven seeks to tap into, a song style where the melody is the rhythm of the words – no more, no less.

It is possible that Example 4.3 remains unfinished because such a song style did not give Beethoven enough to work with, hence the later sketch in triple time from 1820. Yet if one were to take an equivalent four-bar fragment from the beginning of his 'Ode to Joy' tune it would seem similarly blunt and unyielding. A reduction to melodic essentials is clearly a matter to be celebrated within the vast landscape of the Ninth

Symphony. But there is evidence that Beethoven revelled in such *reductio ad nihilum* in song too. His setting of *Der Bardengeist* dates from 1813, the time of *Der Gesang der Nachtigall*, yet it outstrips the Herder setting in taking melody to the edge of musical nothingness. In this case the vocal line suggests little more than inflexions around a monotone, a kind of written out balladic recitation:

Example 4.4 Beethoven *Der Bardengeist*

The substance of the song, in as much as it seeks to comment on the sad tale of loss given by Herrmann's poem, resides mostly in the keyboard's framing of the vocal line, for the keyboardist sets out to sing a song that does not entirely coincide with what the singer produces. The two-bar harp-like pattern of the prelude points up the irregularity that creeps into the vocal line, as the voice's first two-bar shape is unexpectedly extended into a three-and-a-half bar phrase overall. From bar 6 the voice shifts from beginning phrases on the half bar to stressing the downbeat, only for the piano to interrupt and reinstate the half-bar emphasis for the song's postlude. The listener has to decide where to orientate the main melodic statement, whether with the vocal downbeat of bar 6 or with the keyboard accent on the second beat of bar 11. It is not clear which song is primary, the singer's or the keyboardist's, or whether in fact the listener is being offered a dual presentation. Beethoven seems to be invoking the situation in which he finds himself with the Thomson folksong settings, where the vocal melody is given in stone, so to speak, for the composer to arrange instrumentally. In the Thomson settings Beethoven's voice as a composer was by necessity consigned to the instrumental parts, particularly as Thomson did not send him the words of the songs to be arranged. One ends up with a song in the margins of song, Beethoven in dialogue with an unknown singer where the dialogue becomes almost more interesting than the song itself.

Such a model of song, as a potential dialogue between multiple singers, is particularly appropriate for the text of *Der Bardengeist*. Herrmann's poem focusses upon an act of evocation where the listener is invited to tune into a song that the poet hears from a bardic figure that emerges like a ghost out of the past. There are in fact three possible songs that the poet might be offering – his own, the song of the bard which emerges from the fifth verse, or an echo from ancient Teutonia which the bard refers to in the seventh verse:

Dort auf dem hohen Felsen sang
Ein alter Bardengeist;
Es tönt wie Äolsharfenklang
Im bangen schweren Trauersang,
Der mir das Herz zerreist.

Und wie vom Berge zart und lind
Ins süsse Blumenland
Kastalias heil'ge Quelle rinnt:
So wallt und rauscht im Morgenwind
Das silberne Gewand.

Nur leise rauscht sein Lied dahin
Beim grauen Dämmerschein,
Und zu den hellen Sternen hin
Entschwebt sein Herz, sein tiefer Sinn
In süssen Träumerein.

Und still ergriff mich mehr und mehr
Sein wunderbares Lied.
Was siehst du, Geist, so bang und schwer,
Was suchst du dort im Sternenheer?
Wie dir die Seele glüht!

'Ich suche wohl, nicht find' ich mehr,
Ach! Die Vergängenheit.
Ich sehe wohl so bang und schwer,
Ich suche dort im Sternenheer
Der Deutscher goldne Zeit.

Hinunter ging die Sonne schon,
Kaum blieb ein Widerschein;
Mit Arglist und mit frechem Hohn
Pflanzt nun die düstre Nacht den Mohn
Ums Grab der Väter ein.

Ja, herrlich, unerschüttert, kühn
Stand einst der Deutsche da;
Ach! über schwanke Trümmer ziehn
Verhängnisvolle Sterne hin.
Es *war* Teutonia.'

Noch auf dem hohen Felsen sang
Der alter Bardengeist;
Es tönt wie Äolsharfenklang
Ein banger, schwerer Trauersang,
Der mir das Herz zerreist.
                    (Erichson, 1814, 12)

[There on the lofty rock sang
An old bardic spirit;
It sounds like an Aeolian harp
In a fearful heavy lament
That breaks my heart asunder.

And as sweet and soft from the mountain
Into the land of flowers
Runs Castalia's holy spring:
So flows and swells in the morning wind
The silver cloak.

Only lightly swells his song
In the grey dawn light,
And away to the bright stars above
Floats his heart, his deep sense
Sweetly dreaming.

And quietly gripped me more and more
His wondrous song.
Why do you look, Spirit, so fearful and heavy?
What do you seek in the starry host?
How your soul glows within you!

'I truly seek, and no longer find,
Ah, the past.
I truly look, so fearful, so heavy,
I seek there in the starry host
For the Germans' golden time.

The sun was already sinking,
Hardly a reflection remained;
With malice and with insolent scorn
A dark night of poppies grows
Over the grave of our fathers.

Yes, bright, unshaken, brave
The Germans once stood there;
Ah, over the feeble ruins pass
The fateful stars.
It *was* Teutonia'.

Still on the lofty rock sang
The old bardic spirit;
It sounds like an Aeolian harp
A fearful, heavy lament
That breaks my heart asunder.]
                    (Author's translation)

The poem relies upon hearts breaking over the resonance of the 'Trauer-sang' (see verses 1 and 8). If the song fragments are to be drawn together in listeners' experience, it is through their tuning into the basic tone of grieving, as conveyed through the relentless tread of the ballad, the bare iamb. The dislocation of the phrasing in Beethoven's setting detaches the lilting iambs from the melodic fabric so that they lodge as distinct elements in the listener's memory. The singer is invited to rehear them according to the content of each strophe. But in an important sense there is a song complete in the listener's imagination from the keyboard's first intoning of the balladic rhythm.

In one of the poems that Beethoven was not sent when making his folksong arrangements, 'Glencoe' by Walter Scott, the bard is asked who will hear his 'wayward notes of wail and woe, far down the desert of Glen-coe', where the eagle 'from high screams chorus to thy minstrelsy'. The bard answers that his faint strings 'can but sound in desert lone their grey-hair'd master's misery'. The emptiness – both literal and metaphorical – creates resonance. And it is some of that emptiness that Beethoven evokes in *Der Bardengeist*. It might be hard to encourage singers, pianists and lis-teners to invest time in engaging with eight verses of overtly sentimental nationalism. In order to be patient with both Herrmann and Beethoven it helps to remember the Ossianic fervour that gripped the early Roman-tic period, witness Goethe's inclusion of lengthy passages of Ossian for Werther to recite to Lotte in *Die Leiden des jungen Werthers*. But the inter-est of *Der Bardengeist*, for those concerned with what song might have meant to Beethoven, remains indisputable. It is common enough to say that lyric song is about imaginative evocation, but *Der Bardengeist* goes further and makes the listener aware of emptiness. The song goes round and round in circles without seeming to arrive anywhere. As with an Aeolian harp, mentioned in the first and last verses, the different phrases drift on the wind; there is not much distinguishing it from nothingness, except for the call to attention represented by the first iambic lilt.

In Beethoven's second setting of Herder, *Die laute Klage* of 1815, a bal-ladic lilt is associated with the cooing of a turtle dove. Herder alternates trochaic and dactylic rhythms in his poem but Beethoven creates a mes-meric quality out of the single dying fall of 'Turtel', as captured in the repetitions of the keyboard. If one focusses on this underlying tread, then the moans of the dove do indeed seem to outdo the lament of the poet. Music is heard to overshadow the words or, as the poet implies, words are shown to be insufficient to express the depth of internal sorrow:

> Turteltaube, du klagest so laut und raubest dem Armen
> Seinen einzigen Trost, süssen vergessenden Schlaf.

Turteltaub', ich jammer wie du, und berge den Jammer
Ins verwundete Herz, in die verschlossene Brust.
Ach die hartvertheilende Liebe! Sie gab dir die laute
Jammerklage zum Trost, mir den verschlummenden Gram!
(Herder, 1792, 89)

[Turtle dove, you lament so loudly and rob the poor one
Of his only comfort, sweet forgetting sleep:
Turtle dove, I grieve like you and hide the grief
In my wounded heart, in my closed up breast.
Ah, the harsh sharing of love! It gave you
The loud grieving lament for comfort, me the silenced sorrow.]
(Author's translation)

The cooing rhythm comes to a climax in Beethoven's setting of Herder's third couplet 'Ach, die hartvertheilende Liebe!', where hammered diminished sevenths disrupt the voice's melodic flow to dramatic effect. Here the words seem contorted to fit the trochaic rhythms. But in fact from the opening the song is marked by an extreme flexibility in the vocal line, a nuanced declamation which allows the voice to weave around the piano's tread, sometimes seeming to refer to it and sometimes not. The melodic inflexions added to 'laut' and 'Armen' in the second and third bars, and to 'vergessenden Schlaf' at the cadence, weave a veil around the piano's underlying punctuation (see Example 4.5).

Such moments contrast with the voice's insistent return to the 'Turtel' rhythm in bar 6, a return which interrupts the piano's echoes of the previous phrase. As the piano picks up the voice's cue in bar 7, the voice inserts an extra semiquaver rest as though stopping to listen. Beethoven thus creates a subtle dialogue of bird and poet that transcends the immediate demands of word-painting. If the trochaic rhythms represent the object nature of the song, the relentlessness of the lament, then the twisting vocal line represents how listeners must respond with processes of internalisation. By showing how the poet makes the turtle's lament his own Beethoven invites listeners to respond in their turn. Bird and poet come together in the climax of bars 12 and 13, but then the trochaic rhythms appear to fade. After the cadence in bar 17 the marking of the third quaver of the bar, the sound that characterises the dove's call, disappears altogether. Yet the large-scale musical and textual repetition that is introduced from the second half of bar 19 ensures that the trochaic lilt continues. As the passage from bar 17 recurs from bar 24, it becomes clear that the rests are preparing spaces for the cooing to be evoked in the listener's mind. Silence ensures the song.

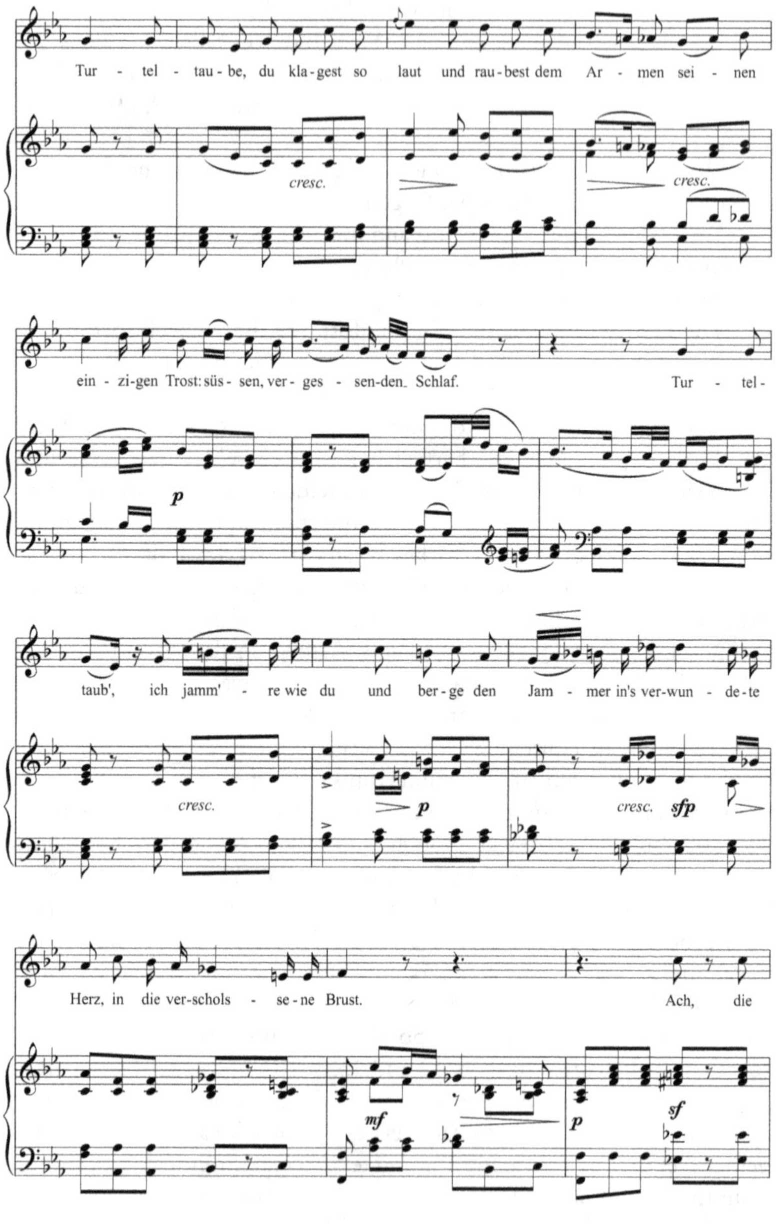

Example 4.5 Beethoven *Die laute Klage*

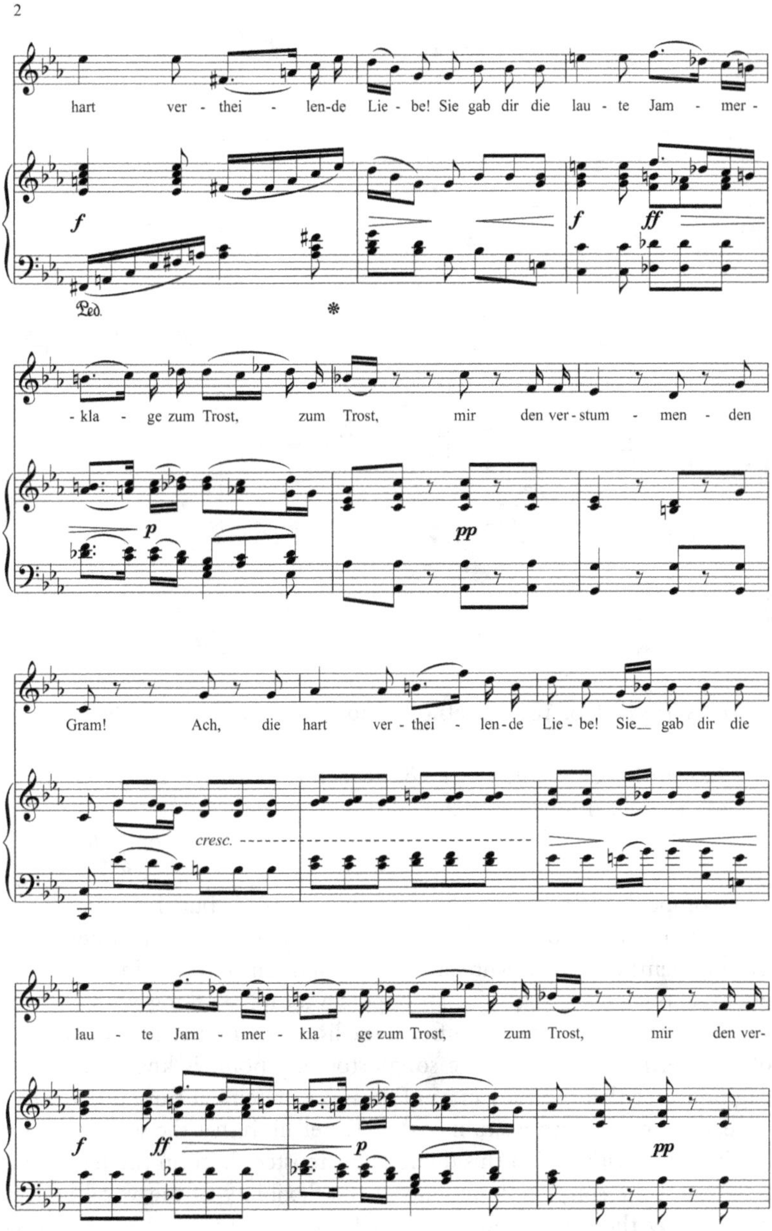

Example 4.5 (Continued)

Example 4.5 (Continued)

In his *Tagebuch* of 1813 Beethoven noted this quote from Herder:

> Learn to keep silent, O friend. Speech is like silver, but to be silent at the right moment is pure gold.
>
> (Solomon, 1988, 247)

The composer set these words as a canon in 1816, but they might also have acted as a motto for his setting of *Die laute Klage* a year earlier. Beethoven seems to have learnt something important in engaging with this poem, about how songs offer an opportunity for working with silence. In its shortness such a song confronts the listener with the absolute nature of closure. It is as though the song's stopping point is known from its beginning, so that the song can unfold as one statement from proposition to realisation. The proposition of the 'Turtel' lilt is that the song will die; the intensity with which this dying fall is resisted, both in the harmonic richness of the song's textures and in the flexibility of the vocal line, is matched by the thoroughness with which any forward impetus is dismantled in the song's final section. Paul Reid points out how Beethoven changes Herder's final words from 'mir den verstummenden Gram' to 'mir den verstummenden Sinn'; 'silenced sense' replaces 'silenced sorrow' as though to encourage reference to the composer's deafness (Reid, 2007, 126). However, this phrase – in either version – is more than personal; it sums up the power of final words within the enclosed nature of song. Their meaning – 'no more can be said' – cuts across the song with the force of a radical twist, even though the meaning was prefigured from the song's opening. Beethoven thus shows his mastery of song as miniature. One is reminded of how Hugo Wolf can illuminate the enclosed patterns of song with one note, as he momentarily separates the voice from the tolling patterns of the piano at the final return to the opening in his setting of *Das verlassene Mägdlein:*

Example 4.6 Wolf *Das verlassene Mägdlein*, bars 5–6

Example 4.7 Wolf *Das verlassene Mägdlein*, bars 38–39

'Thus it is' becomes imbued with 'if only it were different'. Similarly in Beethoven's *Die laute Klage*, the shift in the declamation of 'mir' at the end of the song, from coinciding with the trochaic lilt in bar 24 to stressing the second quaver beat – the sound in between the cooing pulses of the dove – in bar 26, creates an unbearable moment of self-awareness before the postlude's fade into silence.

Wolf was furious if any critic dared focus on the littleness of his songs (Walker, 1968, 236); he viewed their smallness as an opportunity to explore emotional extremes, of a depth that could hold their own with any Wagnerian music drama. He insisted that he was an 'objective lyricist' (Decsey, 1921, 147). Thus the length of one of his songs was what it needed to be in order to convey the nature of the poetic content. If a song was short it was not in order to appeal to the listener's sentimentality. There was for him a crucial aesthetic distinction between an affected miniaturism and a smallness that came through a process of poetic engagement. This distinction might help in understanding the startling difference between Beethoven's two Herder settings, *Der Gesang ger Nachtigall* and *Die laute Klage*. Both songs focus on an evocation of birdsong, but whereas in *Der Gesang der Nachtigall* the imitation of birds creates a folkish charm, in *Die laute Klage* every 'coo' carries the weight of a poetic interpretation. Paul Reid points out that the short prelude that is added to some editions of *Die laute Klage*, to suggest – as in the prelude to *Der Gesang der Nachtigall* – the bird's preliminary chirping, is 'entirely spurious'(Reid, 2007, 126). The concentration of sound and sense in *Die laute Klage* is of a quite different order from word-painting. One might hear echoes of the intensity of Pamina's lament 'Ach ich fühl's' from Mozart's *Die Zauberflöte*; the anguished stretching of the vocal line and the tolling of the trochaic rhythm create a certain emotional kinship. But there is no sense which would characterise this song as an operatic cavatina or cantata, in the fashion of *Adelaide*. In fact, most of the generic distinctions that have been referred to throughout this book – 'Gesang' versus 'Lied', Viennese keyboard song versus North German *im Volkston*, strophic versus through-composed – seem rather irrelevant here. Instead Beethoven gives the impression of seeking a newly distilled version of lyric song. The declamatory nature of the vocal line is perhaps the clearest sign of the depth of his poetic engagement. The overlapping of the instrumental and vocal phrases gives an improvisatory nature to the whole, as though the singer were seeking to pull out words from inside the 'verschlossene Brust'. The poet's inner world is drawn out into melodic expression, just as the outer world of the dove's rhythms becomes more and more internalised.

This turning inside out, or outside in, is one of the most distinctive aspects of the lyric impulse, but rarely does one find it so clearly exposed. The year of Beethoven's *Die laute Klage*, 1815, is often viewed as a time of transition to the composer's late style, and there is much in this song that could be treated as a turning point in the composer's awareness of the potential hidden in each musical detail. It would be tempting to claim that song reveals the heart of Beethoven's late style, or that having reached such a point of stylistic maturity the composer ushered in the era of the German Romantic Lied proper. Yet the picture is hardly so simple. Although, as has been discussed, the Ninth Symphony draws powerfully upon song resources, these are explored and played out as much around song as in song itself. The tension of large versus small remains, as it does in the song-influenced territory of the late string quartets. It is also noticeable that in many of the songs of the late period Beethoven stays close to the stylistic categories that he assumed from other composers. *Der Kuss* of 1822, possibly his last completed song, is a delightful Anacreontic evocation that is reminiscent of the Viennese keyboard song idiom of Mozart and Haydn; according to Paul Reid, the earliest sketches for the song indeed date from 1798 (Reid, 2007, 112). *Abendlied unterm gestirnten Himmel* of 1820 betrays a mood of exaltation more in keeping with the spirit of the Ninth Symphony, but the song's strophic construction and its almost statuesque phrases link it back to Beethoven's Gellert settings, his early tribute to the sublime hymn styles of C. P. E. Bach. One cannot argue that Beethoven left all his earlier song influences behind in his late period, even though he seemed to be delving deeper and deeper into an engagement with poetic words. Yet there is one song from 1817, *Resignation*, that joins *Die laute Klage* in seeming to achieve a new kind of lyric distillation. As Paul Reid points out, *Resignation* makes another reference to one of the Gellert songs, *Die Ehre Gottes der Natur*, in the piano's pulsing chords of bars 17 and 18 (Reid, 2007, 240), but unlike in *Abendlied unterm gestirnten Himmel* the reference is only a snatch. The vocal melody is far from hymn-like in style, being projected as a kind of whispered enunciation. Apart from the performance instruction – *wohl akzentuiert und sprechend vorgetragen* (well accented and performed as if spoken) – Beethoven inserts rests into almost every bar to prevent the voice singing through. This could be seen partly as a word-painting device since the poet likens his life to the flickerings of a candle flame. Beethoven treats 'Lisch aus' (go out) onomatopoeically as the sound of a final sputter. He excerpts the two words before the setting proper begins, as though to identify them as part of the prelude and to establish the poetic meaning of the repeated instrumental motif (see Example 4.8).

Heard in this way the piano prelude goes round in a circle of descending thirds, bar 4 returning to bar 1. The circles continue with bars 9 and 10 returning harmonically to bars 1 and 2, even though bar 10 is offered as a point of vocal cadence. Such circularity magnifies the effect of the song's initial elision of the downbeat, where the harmony changes with

Example 4.8 Beethoven *Resignation*

Example 4.8 (Continued)

the third rather than the first beat of the bar. At first hearing it is almost impossible to know which is stressed, 'Lisch' or 'aus', though the upbeat impetus on 'Lisch' in bar 5 gives the stress to 'aus', on the way to a more definite emphasis on 'Licht' on the downbeat of bar 6. The echoing of this melodic downbeat in bar 10 might seem to offset the harmonic circularity of this opening passage. Yet as the piano adds a further echo, the melodic outline is distilled back to a two-quaver span as in the sputtering of the prelude. Even the resolute setting of 'Du mußt nun los dich binden' (You must now break free), which Beethoven repeats to make a four-bar vocal phrase, appears dangerously stuck on B, the pitch with which the first vocal phrase ended in bar 10. From this vocal pitch in bar 15 the keyboard resumes the falling thirds of the prelude to lead into the no-man's-land of the pulsing chords in bar 17.

Harmonically bars 17 and 18 of *Resignation* are clearly a step into the unknown; it is only in retrospect from the context of the next four-bar phrase that one hears the C major as the subdominant of G, the temporary stopping-point of bar 10. Yet, even more crucially perhaps, these bars signal uncertainty in one's sense of the song's time frame. The textural contrast suggests the end of one section and the readiness for something new, but as one seeks to hear back over the first section each marker collapses back onto the previous one, so that it seems the song proper has yet to begin. The Bs of 'binden' (bar 15) fold back into those of 'finden' and 'Licht' (bars 10 and 6); the falling D-B of 'mein Licht' (bar 5 to bar 6) is absorbed back into the thirds of the prelude. The musical analogy for the sputtering candle is not just traced motivically through the figure of a falling third; it is realised through every aspect of the song down to its most basic formal shaping. The phrase pattern of bars 11 to 15, of two plus two bars, reemerges from bars 19 to 22 and again from bars 23 to 26. Yet rather than building a forward momentum for the song, these phrases once again reveal an obsessive circling around B. The C-B cadential fall for 'Luft entwandt' (bar 22) refers back once more to the C#-B of bar 10, whilst the whole of the next phrase hovers expectantly over the same pitches. The collapse of the phrasing into recitative fragments from bar 26 confirms this waywardness in the song's forward movement. One would hesitate to identify the harmonic or motivic implications of the voice's exposed F#-C# fall in bars 28 to 29; it comes across as an improvised response to the words 'Findet nicht' (does not find). The song falls into silence in the uncomfortable sense of seeming to have lost direction or to have come to a complete halt. The piano's held dominant seventh on A recalls the punctuation of operatic recitative. The pause on the chord in bar 29 cuts off the song's previous sense of rhythmic momentum; the singer has to, as it were, begin again from silence. Yet this is where the essential nature of the song comes into its own, with its previous weaving of vocal melody from the shards of the piano prelude. The uncertainty that surrounds the pause in bar 29 contrasts with the warmth of expectation that surrounds the pause in bar 32. For the voice's sounding of 'lisch aus mein Licht' in bars 29 and 30, with its echo of bars 5 and 6, confirms that such fragments can be remembered as song. For all its transient patchiness, where the gaps between notes might seem more prominent than the notes themselves, the song's first melodic line returns in full splendour from the end of bar 32. The new phrase that is added from bars 39 to 41 follows the rhythms of bars 11 to 13 but pins them to an emphasis on the tonic D, leading into a fully resolved statement of the opening preludial sequence.

One might expect such a song to end by fading into nothing, the composer extinguishing sound in sympathy with the poet's references to the extinguishing of the light. Beethoven does ask the performers for a continuing *ritenuto* and a *diminuendo* to *pianissimo*. But as the song closes on the melodic A-F#, the fall with which it began, the overriding impression is of sound retained. This seems very much Beethoven's personal interpretation of Haugwitz's poem. When Haugwitz speaks of 'breaking free' he clearly makes a not-so-veiled reference to the rest found in death; his command 'lisch aus' thus implies a need for passive acceptance:

> Lisch aus, mein Licht!
> Was dir gebricht,
> Das ist nun fort,
> An diesem Ort
> Kannst du's nicht wieder finden!
> Du must nun los dich binden.
> Sonst hast du lustig aufgebrannt,
> Nun hat man dir die Luft entwandt;
> Wenn diese fortgewehet,
> Die Flamme irre gehet,
> Sucht – findet nicht –
> Lisch aus, mein Licht!
> (Fouqué, 1817, 256)

> [Go out, my light!
> What you need,
> That has now gone,
> In this place
> You cannot find it again!

> You must now break free.
> Once you used to burn so brightly,
> Now your air has been removed;
> If this blows away,
> The flame collapses
> Seeks – does not find –
> Go out, my light!]
>> (Author's translation).

Beethoven's interpretation of 'lisch aus' – as reflected in the large-scale return of his song's opening section as well as the smaller scale repetitions – seems much more active, as though he were seeking to find new meaning with each re-utterance. In exploring the individual resonance of these two words, particularly of the unusual sounding 'lisch', Beethoven indicates a regeneration of sound and thus a kind of life that fills silences even where they threaten to be absolute. The composer's comment on the sketch of *Resignation* suggests an appeal to performers to face out those silences: 'with intimate feeling, yet resolutely, well accented, and sung as though spoken' (Kramer, 1999, 67). An internal expansion of resonance relies upon the nuances of the voice in performance; while such nuances come from words, in the end they cannot be expressed by them. The lyric impulse in *Resignation* leaps out even from perusing it on the page, but such a song needs to be picked up and sung – and that in the end is what this book seeks to encourage.

References

Beethoven, Ludwig van. *Letters*, tr. and ed. Alfred Christlieb Kalischer, John South Shedlock and Arthur Eaglefield Hull. New York: Dover, 1972.

Cooper, Barry. *Beethoven's Folksong Settings*. Oxford: Clarendon Press, 1994.

Decsey, Ernst. *Hugo Wolf: Das Leben und das Lied*. Berlin, Germany: Schuster and Loeffler, 1921.

Erichson, Hermann J. *Musen-Almanach für das Jahr 1814*. Vienna, Austria: Carl Gerold, 1814.

Fouqué, Friedrich Heinrich Karl de la Motte. *Frauentaschenbuch für das Jahr 1817*. Nuremberg, Germany: J.L. Schrag, 1817.

Gelbart, Matthew. *The Invention of 'Folk Music' and 'Art Music': Emerging Categories from Ossian to Wagner*. Cambridge: Cambridge University Press, 2007.

Glass, Frank. *The Fertilizing Seed: Wagner's Concept of the Poetic Intent*. Ann Arbor, MI: UMI Studies in Musicology, 1983.

Goethe, Johann Wolfgang von. *Selected Verse*, ed. David Luke. Harmondsworth: Penguin Books, 1986.

Hamburger, Michael (ed.). *Beethoven: Letters, Journals and Conversations*. London: Thames and Hudson, 1951.

Hanslick, Eduard. *Music Criticisms 1846–99*, ed. and tr. Henry Pleasants. Harmondsworth: Penguin Books, 1963.

Herder, Johann Gottfried. *Von Deutscher Art und Kunst*. Hamburg, Germany: Bode, 1773.

Herder, Johann Gottfried. *Zerstreute Blätter*. Gotha, Germany: Carl Wilhelm Ettinger, 1792.

Jacobs, Robert L. (tr.). *Three Wagner Essays*. London: Ernst Eulenberg, 1979.

Johnson, Julian. *Mahler's Voice*. Oxford: Oxford University Press, 2009.

Kinderman, William. *Beethoven*. Oxford: Clarendon Press, 1995.

Kramer, Richard. 'Lisch aus mein Licht': Song, Fugue and the Symptoms of a Late Style. *Beethoven Forum* 7, 1999: 67–88.

Mitchell, Donald. *Mahler: The Wunderhorn Years*. London: Faber, 1975.

Nottebohm, Gustav. *Beethoveniana*. Leipzig, Germany: Peters, 1872.

Nottebohm, Gustav. *Zweite Beethoveniana*. Leipzig, Germany: Peters, 1887.

Reichardt, Johann Friedrich. An junge Künstler. In *Musikalisches Kunstmagazin 1*. Berlin, Germany, 1782.

Reid, Paul. *The Beethoven Song Companion*. Manchester: Manchester University Press, 2007.

Solomon, Maynard. *Beethoven Essays*. Cambridge, MA: Harvard University Press, 1988.

Sternfeld, Frederick. *Goethe and Music: A List of Parodies*. New York: New York Public Library, 1954.

Wagner, Richard. *My Life*, ed. Mary Whittall, tr. Andrew Gray. Cambridge: Cambridge University Press, 1983.

Wagner, Richard. *Pilgrimage to Beethoven and Other Essays*, tr. William Ashton Ellis. Lincoln and London: University of Nebraska Press, 1994.

Wagner, Richard. *Opera and Drama*, tr. William Ashton Ellis. Lincoln and London: University of Nebraska Press, 1995.

Walker, Frank. *Hugo Wolf*. London: Dent, 1968.

Conclusion

Beethoven's song *Resignation* is a poignant reminder that the lyric impulse may spring from words but in the end cannot be confined by them, or even captured by them. The direction of lyric impulses is always away from their source and towards the response of the next singer in the lyric chain. In a letter to Charlotte von Stein of 1786, Goethe tells an anecdote of hearing gondoliers singing to each other across the waters of the lagoon in Venice:

> The farther they are from each other, the more delightful the song, and between the two is the best spot for the listener. . . . I walked up and down between them, always away from the one whose turn it was to sing and towards the one who was stopping. . . . This tune over whose dead notes we have often puzzled in vain, now seems so alive to me, this song that one solitary man sends into the distance for another who feels as he does, to hear and answer him.
>
> (Herzfeld, 1957, 178)

Goethe confirms that it is the waiting on response that enlivens song, though he places himself one step ahead of the next singer in line by walking towards the one who will hear what the next singer sings. The poet aligns himself with silence rather than sound, with the 'one who was stopping', but that place of fragility brings the song alive. It makes the listener strain to hear what might otherwise be merely 'dead notes'.

One might imagine such a model of enlivened song being acted out between Goethe and Zelter, his closest composer friend. Goethe said Zelter's music caught the essence of his poetry and lifted it up like hot air within a balloon (Hecker, 1913, 59; Byrne Bodley, 2009, 266); but then his melodies would inspire Goethe to further poetic flights in his turn. Within the salon environment of the Goethe circle, poetry and music spawned multiple reflections, a kind of lyric contagion. It is an environment that Goethe clearly felt was threatened by the urgency of Beethoven's particular composer persona; he said he had never experienced an artist 'so concentrated, so forceful, with such depth of feeling' (Herzfeld, 1957, 375). In many senses Beethoven found himself outside such circles of intimate exchange. One does not hear of Beethoven's songs being shared in the kind of salon environments enjoyed by Hugo Wolf in the Vienna *Wagnerverein*, or more famously by Schubert at the home of Joseph von Spaun. His seems a lone voice by comparison – whether from choice, or from his songs being often so difficult to sing. Yet returning to Goethe's model of lyric enlivenment, being at a distance should not of itself inhibit the working of the lyric impulse. Much as one might be interested in the motivations and contexts for Beethoven's song-writing, the key question becomes not the composer's intentions in his songs but whether singers want to sing them and what listeners find themselves hearing in them – and that can only be established in the action of singing.

In his book *The Composer's Voice*, Edward Cone guides performers through the complexities of Schubert's setting of *Erlkönig* with the notion that they should be seeking to utter the composer's voice, to make a kind of virtual persona for him out of their performance choices (Cone, 1974, 5). According to Cone there is a drama of impersonation that takes place in the performance of song. Such a model draws on a sense of completeness and acknowledged excellence in what the composer has provided. Cone places performers and listeners in the role of decoders or interpreters of finished business. From such a viewpoint Beethoven's songs create an unfair burden, since they are so often elusive, ambiguous, even fragmentary. The material Beethoven offers in his setting of *Der Bardengeist* points away from itself to other possible songs. Phrasing begins, breaths are taken, but they peter out before the implied circumference of the strophe is fully realised. At the other extreme, a song like Beethoven's second setting of *An die Hoffnung* provides too much material, spilling over with a proliferation of vocal twists and turns from which the performer-listener must extract an essence; the song has yet to be made. Yet from the point of view of the lyric impulse, this places energy exactly where it should be, with what a respondent – whether listener or performer – will seek to do next. Beethoven's songs belong far more aptly with Carolyn Abbate's view of 'potentially multiple musical voices' inhabiting a work than with Cone's insistence on a 'monophonic, single 'voice'' (Abbate, 1991, x, 251). And yet it would be misleading to describe such voices as remaining 'unsung' in the Abbate sense. There is a song to be sung, it is just one is always waiting in eager anticipation for the next performer-listener to do so. There is a sequencing to this multiplicity of voice, as one example of unfinished business – from poet to composer – provokes further unfinished business between composer, performer and listener. As in Goethe's model of singing across the Venetian lagoon, there is an urgency that one singer should affirm that something has been heard that can be passed on, even across an intervening silence. In Goethe's anecdote the chain involves only two singers, but since each is isolated and works across distance, relying on the sympathy of the next singer to keep the responses coming, the chain could be extended almost indefinitely once a response has been logged – once the 'I sing' has received the response 'I hear that you sing'.

Much of the content of this book has been devoted to amassing evidence that Beethoven did indeed hear the voice of some of the poets that he set – even the voice of Goethe with whom he had a fairly tempestuous relationship. Yet my detailed commentaries of individual songs could more accurately be described as kinds of performance, seeking to fashion my responses to the ingredients of each song into a pattern of voice that might provoke further soundings. There is nothing pure about this process. My sense of song ingredients has been greatly influenced by Beethoven performers – singers and pianists – and by other listeners' reactions. In a sense a commentator's words can only ever catch onto performers' coat tails. As George Steiner says:

> No musicology, no music criticism, can tell us as much as the action of meaning which is performance. . . . Unlike the reviewer, the literary critic, the academic vivisector and judge, the executant invests his own being in the process of interpretation. His readings, his enactments of chosen meanings and values are not those of eternal survey. They are a commitment at risk, a response which is, in the root sense, responsible.
>
> (Steiner, 1992, 22)

The risk of investing in the moment, with all its transience, is exactly what the lyric impulse requires. Such moments do not last in the sense of 'eternal survey', but they do accelerate processes of reaction and counter-reaction within the liveliness of a lyric chain. That chain cannot be sustained merely by a look back to origins, but relies upon future responses, future performances. The commitment of performers, and listeners to performances, is vital if a lyric chain is to gather voice and not fall silent. Some might feel that performing Beethoven's songs is not worth the effort, or that a lyric chain never really took off in this instance. But this is where a commentator might have a role to play, bearing witness to a lyric chain in action – evoking where it has been and where it might lead next.

References

Abbate, Carolyn. *Unsung Voices*. Princeton, NJ: Princeton University Press, 1991.

Byrne Bodley, Lorraine (ed.). *Goethe and Zelter: Musical Dialogues*. London: Ashgate, 2009.

Cone, Edward. *The Composer's Voice*. Berkeley, CA: University of California Press, 1974.

Hecker, Max (ed.), *Der Briefwechsel zwischen Goethe and Zelter*. Volume 1. Leipzig, Germany: Insel Verlag, 1913.

Herzfeld, Marianne von (ed.). *Letters from Goethe*, tr. Marianne von Herzfeld anhin the setting Reichd C. Melvil Sym. Edinburgh: Edinburgh University Press, 1957.

Steiner, George. *Real Presences*. London: Faber, 1992.

Index

Hoffmann, E. T. A. 1, 3
Hölty, Ludwig Christoph Heinrich 47, 88–91

Lessing, Gottfried Ephraim 37, 42, 44

Mahler, Gustav 9, 118–120
Matthisson, Friedrich von 59–65, 91–93
Mozart, Wolfgang Amadeus 36, 138–139; *Die Zauberflöte* 39, 53–54, 138

Reichardt, Johann Friedrich 16–18, 20, 47, 99, 123–125, 127; 'Kennst du das Land' 16–18
Reissig, Christian Ludwig 65–67, 69, 72, 82
Rochlitz, Friedrich 4

Schiller, Johann Christoph Friedrich von 6, 36–39, 53, 82–84, 90–91, 123
Schlegel, Friedrich 97
Schopenhauer, Arthur 1, 11
Schubert, Franz 36–37, 90, 99, 127, 147
Schulz, Johann Abraham Peter 23, 123–125
Schumann, Robert 36
Spohr, Louis 16, 20
Staiger, Emil 6, 82–84, 90–91
Sulzer, Johann Georg 96

Tieck, Ludwig 1–3, 38

Wagner, Richard 1, 112, 114, 116–117
Wolf, Hugo 9, 137–138, 147

Zelter, Carl Friedrich 59, 99, 146

For Product Safety Concerns and Information please contact our EU
representative GPSR@taylorandfrancis.com
Taylor & Francis Verlag GmbH, Kaufingerstraße 24, 80331 München, Germany